IDENTIFi YOURSELF

A JOURNEY IN F**K YOU CREATIVE COURAGE

STUART S. SHAPIRO

Waterside Press

DEDICATION

To my wonderful wife, Laurie Dolphin,

My Partner,

My Muse,

My Love,

My cherished designer.

How lucky can I get?

Her art of contextual design has given poetry to my words.

So Special.

So Thankful

So much in Love

THE DALAI LAMA, WHEN ASKED WHAT SURPRISED HIM THE MOST ABOUT HUMANITY ANSWERED "Man. He sacrifices his health in order to make money. Then he sacrifices money to recuperate his health. And then he is so anxious about the future that he does not enjoy the present:

THE RESULT BEING THAT HE DOES NOT LIVE IN THE PRESENT OR THE FUTURE; HE LIVES AS IF HE IS NEVER GOING TO DIE, AND THEN DIES HAVING NEVER LIVED."

—H.H. THE DALAI LAMA

THE MEANING OF LIFE IS TO FIND OUT WHO YOU ARE

—DEEPAK CHOPRA

TABLE OF CONTENTS

WOODSTOCK'S SMELL OF FREEDOM IN 1999 WAS SIMILAR IN AUGUST 1968, when Czechoslovakia was free and they were dancing in the streets, even though the country knew its freedom was going to end as soon as the Soviets decided to bust the poor bastards for having too good of a time. Freedom? You want Free Man? Fuck You!

NOT TOO MUCH DIFFERENT.

So why do we always get busted after having too good of a time?

What does this tell us about our identity?

What do I want to be?

Who do I want to be?

Who am I in my own image?

Who am I?

In the Image of

My Father

My Mother

My Boss

The Judge,

Before whom I am trying to wiggle out of a misdemeanor?

Most important is:

WHAT DO I WANT TO FEEL IN THE MORNING WHEN I AWAKE?

AM I PROUD OF MYSELF, IN THOSE EARLY MOMENTS OF CLARITY?

DO I SNAP OUT OF BED AND
CAN'T WAIT TO BE WHO I AM THAT DAY?
DOES THE PERSON I AWAKE NEXT TO
GIVE ME
STRENGTH AND
SUPPORT

Or

Do I drag my sorely ass out of bed

To go to work for some fuck who

Scares me and

Terrorizes my self-esteem and personal trajectory?

Do I kick butt

Or

Do I get my ass kicked everyday by my boss and fellow workers?

Am I content with the person I wake up with, and

Turn to him or her with

Affection

Love

Or

Do I bolt away, in

Fear of touching intimacy that

Scares my inner heart?

Do I wake up, and my first thought is that of
Someone else I may be cheating with instead of
Loving my wife or partner at my side with
Affection and Pride?

Am I still horny for someone I saw in a movie or
Fantasized about on the street?
And when I embrace my lover
Am I obsessed with that fantasy?

AM I HAPPY AND WANT TO BE ME,

Or
Am I immediately scared of dragging into another day, with
Contempt for the daily process of life and
The lack of pursuit of
My personal evolution and
Success?

Do I revel in the love of my life and
The excitement of making a million nano-decisions that
Envelope the Excitement of
An Active Life in
Pursuit of my Evolution and Growth?

Is the Moment,

The Day-to-Day,

The Love of the Decision,

The intuitive ability to be able to have an immediate

Cause and Effect

Point and

Centerfold of

My Health and

Wealth

A Natural State of Being?

AM I THE DEER CAUGHT IN THE HEADLIGHTS OF MY OWN INERTIA FOR
FEAR OF MAKING THE WRONG DECISION?

Do I allow the concern for the

Downsize Risk to

Constantly Outweigh the

Willingness to

Jump with Confidence,

Knowing that

Sometimes.

Many Times.

I can still be wrong?

Am I confused inside by the
Fringes of
Right and
Wrong?
The Ebbs and Flows of
The Beats in Both Directions?

How do I learn the
Lessons that my
Father wanted to teach me, but I was
Too Rebellious to Embrace?
Until I finally reached the magical age, and
Had my own son, and
Finally realized it was OK to actually embrace
Who and
What
My Father was and
What He stood for.
What he was Teaching Me
About Life and the
Pursuit of Happiness.

Am I
The Internet of One and All?
Connected to the
Universal Knowledge with

A Click and Touch that is Me,
Within the Body of
My community as the center of
My experience and
Travel and
Exploration?

Do I Fear
The Quest of Knowledge because
It is too Labor-Intensive and
Requires the Freedom of Self-Discovery?

Can I
Instantaneously Travel Somewhere,
Anywhere,
With a simple Click of my Heart and Soul,
Aided by whatever Tools I have at my disposal—
And Those that I have to Stretch for?

DO I GET STUCK IN
THE FEAR OF
MISSING A LOST OPPORTUNITY THAT
I FALSELY THINK WILL REAPPEAR?

Well
My
Son and
Sons
Daughters,
Night Flighters,
Constituents,
Long Lost Lovers,
Soul Mates,
Lost Mates,
Living and
Dead
Brothers
Sisters
Mothers
Fathers
The Living Legacy and
Luck of our Time is that

NEVER BEFORE HAS THE WORLD BEEN SO ALIVE WITH OPPORTUNITY, AVAILABLE TO THE INDIVIDUAL WHIMS OF OUR SEARCHING SOULS

And Never Before have we all been
So Lucky
To Experience the World
Inside and Out,
Above and Below,
Outside the Galaxy,
Inside the Black Holes of Life
With such
Reckless Abandonment,
Without Reprisal,
And with
Endless Courage.

THE FREEDOM TO LIVE A CREATIVE AND FULFILLING LIFE BASED ON WHO WE ARE AT OUR CORE WHO WE WANT TO GROW TO BE FROM OUR SOUL HAS NEVER BEEN MORE COMPELLING AND EASIER TO ACHIEVE.

I Hope and Pray
These Nuggets of Wisdom of a
69-year-Old-Youngling with an
Old Evolution will Yield
Strength and
Security.

To Deliver
Comfort
Strength
Courage

To Give Extra
Baseline Courage
To Explore
Embrace
Take Control of
Your Boundaries and
Break Them Down

And
Create New Ones
Throughout
Your Life,
To Grow
Stronger
Healthier

WITHOUT FEAR
OF CONSEQUENCE
SUCCESS OR FAILURE
TO HARNESS
THE CREATIVE
COURAGE OF
YOUR IDENTITY
TO CONSTRUCT YOUR OWN
FOUNDATIONAL PLATFORM,
ENABLING SECURITY AND
FREEDOM OF CHOICE.

IN THE BEGINNING…
I was a Skinny Jewish Kid
in a small mill town
with buckteeth, curly hair
and a Wise Ass personality.
Getting into fights and
being chased home from school
was a daily routine.

I KNEW I WAS DIFFERENT

Not because I was a Jew and
A rich kid in a
working class town,
North Adams
but
Because
I had a Punkie outlook that was clearly different
from everyone else's.

Luck and thoughtful parents got me out of what was called
the Normal School and into
Private education all the way through college and
I never looked back.

My Cutting Edge tendencies started pretty early.
I was always the social chairman and my first production was
the prom dance in prep school. Asked to book the normal,
boring high school band in 1964,
I opted for the school's first taste of a Rock and Roll Band.
As the band lit up the room with screaming guitars,
It was the first of many times in my life I heard:

"DO YOU KNOW WHAT YOU'VE DONE?"

It became my lifelong mantra.

Until I finally grew up at 50, and went to work in Congress

Mr. Technology

An architect of Constituent Internet Communication.

No one would have ever bet that Mister Late Night Cult Meister

Would have ever turned the leaf to Mr. Shapiro Goes

to Washington.

My favorite-of-all-time "Do you know what you've done?"

was in the screening room of Universal Pictures.

It was 1978 and they had one of the initial press screenings

of *Animal House.*

My friend was handling some radio promotions at the time

and I was releasing the X-Rated, soon to be R-Rated,

animated parody *Tarzoon, Shame of the Jungle.*

My friend slipped the projectionist some cash and he put the

trailer of *Tarzoon* ahead of *Animal House.* The trailer was off

the charts, over-the-top hilarious and very rude and everyone

was caught by surprise, thinking that Universal was going off

the edge.

I was promptly ushered off the lot.

One of my favorite epilogues of "Do you know what you've

done?" was at Woodstock 99.

I produced the live Internet feed from the start of the festival until the last act. The famous fires started quickly by the end of the last performance on the main stage.

The live cable feed went off the air after the last songs, but we were still live on the Internet at Woodstock.com, where the outside world first learned of the Woodstock fire celebration.

Then the moment came and someone with serious authority starting screaming you must stop broadcasting live, fearing the world would find out about the fires and ruin Woodstock Peace and Love. I encouraged my crew to persevere and keep the show going. After all, it was a breakthrough Internet moment for the ages.

Trying to tip over our production truck to make us stop I could hear those magic words of personal success:

"DO YOU REALIZE WHAT YOU HAVE JUST DONE?"

It was a truly paradoxical moment to end the largest Internet festival in history with such a historic feat of Rock and Roll destruction and jubilation.

FOR MUCH OF MY EARLY LIFE I LOOKED FORWARD TO **WHAT I CALLED MOONING CREATIVELY IN PUBLIC.**

I don't believe I had to cultivate this part of my personality.
It was more a case of satisfying a hunger,

A THIRST TO BREAK THE MOLD
TO JUMP OFF THE CREATIVE EDGE

To Give Sunlight to the Crankier Side of Entertainment.

It took its own turn in the '70s into a drugs culture
and continued until
One day, when I was in my 50s,
I realized that I really did not have to force myself to
Pursue a Cutting Edge.
I, like a Painter,
Had my own
Natural State of Style.
No matter what I created
Would Naturally Gravitate to the Outer Edge of Creative Taste.

This Realization freed me from forcing myself to
Prove I was
Cool and
Hip and
Gave me Security in
My Own Creative Identity.
That it was a Natural, Organic Foundation Inside.

Who I was

Was a Natural Process

I did not have

To Fight

To Push

To find the Edge of my Taste

I was the Edge

To Myself and By Myself.

But it didn't start out that way.

AMAZING HOW LONG IT TAKES FOR WISDOM TO SET IN. AND STILL HOW FUCKED UP YOU CAN BE WITH A LITTLE TOUCH OF WISDOM.

In 1978, in the heyday of independent distribution,
I started one of the first video labels, Harmony Vision.
We released a handful of classics: the first ever home videos
of *Pink Flamingos*, *The Hills Have Eyes*, *Jimi Plays Berkley*,
Pinks Floyd's Live at Pompeii. It's hard to imagine today
how over the top Pink Flamingos was in 1978!

Our format of video distribution was pretty unique. I would travel around the country, and with my partner, the infamous video visionary Norman Smith, we would visit my video distributors. We would give them a three-quarter-inch video master so they could make their own VHS cassettes and we only sold them the box covers as the royalty and content. It was a pure Mom and Pop deal, and we never had to worry about royalties getting paid. When they were out of box covers we got paid for more deliveries.

My *Night Flight* story has in it the true sense of the essence of this book. I had been distributing rock and roll, cult, and horror films theatrically under my film company International Harmony.

In the 1970s, we were very successful at midnight screenings for many of the classics. It was keenly obvious that kids were going to the theaters from midnight to 2 AM and were interested in something different, musical and progressive. Back in the Daze, you could get high inside the theater and of course for our kind of movies that was an essential experience.

Stella, my wife at that time, and I were living in Manhattan, and Manhattan Cable was in its very early years. As it turns out, they started to play reruns of women's tennis at midnight on Friday and Saturday.

It was a Clear and Simple Exercise of
Extension of a Platform to a New, Under-Developed
And Under-Delivered Platform.

► **TRANSPOSE THE EXPERIENCE**
► **RECOGNIZE THE HOLE IN THE MARKET**
► **FILL THE HOLE IN THE DISTRIBUTION ECO-SYSTEM**

So I approached my friend, Rock and Roll Agent Extraordinaire, Jeff Franklin, who had a hunger to do more and be more than an agent. Together, we pitched USA Network for a three month, two-hour open time slot on Friday and Saturday, starting at 11 PM. And off we were
Command Central for a Music Video and
Cultural Cable TV revolution

BLESS THE 1980'S

► **HERE'S THE KEY**
CONVERT
LEVERAGE
TRANSPOSE

We recognized there was an undelivered and under-served audience of Night Flighters that wanted to get late night entertainment on their cable TV, in their homes, where they could get high with their friends and sometimes even in front of their younger brothers. It was a stoner time and I understood that the late-night time slot carried with it, in its natural DNA, the need to be something different.

A window to a Brave New World where the earth was not only round, but had a real cutting edge of emerging popular culture that was exploding around us.

A Natural Marriage
Of Time
Structure
Platform
Content Architecture

TIME MATTERS
What Time of Day

Did you know why movies were only 90 minutes long
back in the day?
The seats were hard, and people couldn't sit any longer on them
without getting tired and bored with the movie experience.
So when the seats got cushy the movies could get longer.

It's easy to draw lines between the cable revolution in the '80s and the Internet one of today.

Every day, there is a new start-up that is building out in the holes of the universe.
Some are only obvious once a creative force is applied to the Ah-ha Moment.
But they are there, all day long.

THE BASIC CYCLES EXIST IN EVERY PLATFORM BOTH OLD AND NEW.

THE MOON COMES OUT

AT NIGHT EVEN THOUGH IT IS THERE ALL THE TIME

EVERY TIME JIMI HENDRIX
CAME OFF STAGE he was always very
critical of his performance, saying
how poorly he played and how many
mistakes he made.
Jimi never thought he was good enough,
Even though he knew without doubt,
He was one of God's special angels.
The moment that Jimi played
a single note
He transformed into magic.

THE VERY TOUCH OF HIS FINGER ON A STRING WOULD TRANSFORM AND TRANSFIX EVERYONE INCLUDING HIMSELF.

The harmonic connectivity provided through the
Internet of the universe has never been stronger.
The moment and the realization of that
Power for the individual is unique in history.

This power enables us to realize a sense of
Personal fulfillment in real time.

DO NOT BE DUPED BY THE FALSE HOPE THAT THE FULFULLMENT OF REACHING A GOAL HAS A PAYOFF THAT IS REALLY REWARDING. IT IS NOT SO.

The actual rewards that matter are the
Momentary realizations that you are in the
Process of action.

MOTION IS LIFE
LIFE IS MOTION

Consistency focused on motion will provide all the primary
Foundations of success in the big picture.

STAY IN MOTION

Stay At Bat in the Game

This is where the importance of
Your Identity and the
Security of your
Force Field come into play.

WHAT YOU DO
IS WHO YOU ARE

Fear Not

Like Jimi

THE CREATIVE ROAD NO MATTER HOW GENIUS, IS LITTERED WITH FAILURE AND DISAPPOINTMENT.

Jimi gave us the greatest guitar performances in history yet
He was always self-critical in his pursuit of perfection.
Motion was his Game!

The Greatest hitters of all time in baseball
Only hit at best 40%.
Strikeouts are part of life.
Babe Ruth in his day was the all-time Strike Out King.

Let's assume that you already believe that

WHAT YOU DO IS WHO YOU ARE. WHO YOU ARE IS WHY YOU ARE DOING WHAT YOU DO.

And you are unrestricted in the pursuit of working
within your force field.
Only Then,
The comfort zone of your nature is a natural process.

To be in tune with your natural process is
The foundation of the exercise of life and
The evolution of your talent base.

THE PURSUIT OF A SUCCESSFUL AND HEALTHY LIFE IS TO BECOME WHO AND WHAT YOU ARE IN THE DAY TO DAY PROCESS

There can be no difference between
The person who wakes up in those first moments
And the one who goes to work,
And the one who makes all those decisions all day,
To lie down at night with a sense of
Completion and
Fulfillment with the day and all its madness.

This is a simple process of exercising.

When you play a sport you like,
When you are having fun,
Time goes fast.
The Greater the Impact

When you play life and
Work at a life-sport of job that you love, the same holds true.
Life is more fulfilling.
More rewarding.
More successful.

THAT'S THE GOAL.

► THE UNENDING PURSUIT
OF THE MOMENT OF TRANSITION
TO THE NEXT MOMENT.
**STAY IN MOTION AND HAVE NO FEAR
OF THE STRIKEOUT.
IT ONLY MAKES ROOM FOR THE NEXT
HOME RUN.
THE NEXT GREAT PERFORMANCE.**

IMAGINE, 1968, A JUNIOR IN COLLEGE AT THE HEIGHT OF YOUTHFUL PASSION. A college kid, still being supported by my parents. I was keenly aware of the personal freedom I was about to jump into: spending a whole year in Europe, going to school, learning about European life, culture, history, and the art of personal expression. And smoking the best Hash of a lifetime.

EVEN THOUGH I WAS "THE BABY" BORN TO OLDER PARENTS.

Even though I was a punk and
A rich kid, studied in the pursuit of personal freedom
in prep school.
Even though I had taken acid and survived.
Even though I had hitchhiked back and forth through the States.

I NEVER REALLY FELT THE SURGE OF FREEDOM UNTIL I TOOK MY JUNIOR YEAR ABROAD.

My junior year in 1968 was a defining Life Cycle Moment
in so many ways.

I started out working in an international work camp in Sweden
where I spent the first four weeks building a roof on a Tower of
Babel barn with thirteen nations of boys and girls just like me.

Eighteen years old.
Not a clue about the the world

And the meaning of life.

The beginning head rush of Vietnam.

A month before Czechoslovakia is crushed by an Evil Empire.

Riots in the streets of Paris by angry youth with a

Passionate vision of a better future.

Drugs were never more powerful and impactful.

POLITICS WERE A REAL CASE OF LIFE AND DEATH AND FREEDOM

—or the lack of it—for any young American.

The Draft was Fuckin' Real for All of Us!

I remember the collision of the forces between two of my Czech friends in the work camp in Sweden, even before I arrived in Czechoslovakia.

One:

A Communist,

Who believed in his heart that

Russia and Socialist Communism were

The Right Way.

The Only Way.

The other:

My dear friend Zdenek from Slovakia,

Older and Wiser
Who knew about freedom because he did not feel that he had
any under Communism.
If you could not leave your country freely,
You had a big fucking problem.

As an American,
I really could not relate to Zdenek's sense of political suffering
as an individual.
After the Swedish work camp, I hitchhiked through Poland and
East Germany and over to Czechoslovakia and made my way
to a small town six kilometers from the Russian border.

I was the only American for hundreds of miles and at that time,
America was honored as a Great Country,
Where everyone wanted to live.

AMERICAN LIBERTY AND FREEDOM
WAS MORE OBVIOUS BACK IN THOSE DAYS.

The Czechs were running around in the streets feeling alive
as a people and a culture for the first time in decades.
I never to this day have ever felt such a liberated sense of
freedom like the Czechs enjoyed for that brief moment in time.
Guess it was their Junior Year Abroad.

So here was a country full of

Vibrant,

Exciting,

Free,

Loving people

and then in just one day

The tanks roll in and everything is taken away.

Was it just a question of being able to have

Your own country and

Control of your own personal sense of freedom and

The free expression of your politics?

What is the price of freedom in the land of 5,000 TV channels?

WHAT IS THE PRICE OF ALLOWING OURSELVES TO BE DUPED INTO BELIEVING THAT WE NEED TO GO TO WAR FOR THAT PROTECTION OF FREEDOM?

Where does our culture and politics of personal information
and
Protection of Rights and information intersect today?
Are the total losses of privacy by both government and
corporations a worthy price of our Internet Freedom?

Here's the point:
All our life we will be intoxicated in various ways and exposed
to platforms from
Drugs to Doctors
Parents to Politicians
Psychics to Psychos

What's important is to be able to step away and
Feel your own center of
Sense and Reason
Not with the outside influences
But with your Inside Natural Influences.

TRUST YOUR INSTINCTS.

Hold out *and*
Hold back the
Urges that collaborate with intoxication.

With the rapid ability to shoot off an email without thinking
of how it will be perceived by the receiver,
We have to be more cautious than ever.
Have to learn physical control of fingers on the keyboards.

Continuously update our relationships between
Getting High and
Being Intoxicated.

WHEN I GRADUATED FROM COLLEGE
IN 1970, THE HEAT OF THE VIETNAM WAR
WAS ALL AROUND.
The year before, the draft by the
numbered lottery ranked me high enough
to stay out of the war. Nevertheless,
I made a commitment to myself
that I was never going to allow myself
to be drafted and put into the
armed forces.

I HAD DECIDED TO EITHER MOVE TO CANADA OR GO TO JAIL AND WAS PREPARED TO DO WHATEVER IT TOOK TO STAY OUT.

It was not just that I hated and did not believe in the war,
but I knew in my heart and soul that the experience would
permanently change my life in ways I was unwilling to accept.
Years later, after having several Viet Vets as good friends,
it was obvious to me I was right about the permanent psychic
change and spiritual damage that was unavoidable to anyone who
had the grave misfortune of participating in any war
and in particular the Vietnam War.

WAR IS IMMORAL AND IT SPREADS ITS WRATH TO ALL IN CONTACT AND BEYOND.

Times were different then and I have asked many of my friends
what they thought categorized those days.
Freedom,
Youthful abandonment,
Unified conviction that we were willing to

Stand up and
Fight for what we thought was right against the will of the
government, and
The inspiration that we as a youth movement were going to
Change the world to make a better place all around.

I remember the passion and emotions that Nixon, Mitchell,
and LBJ brought out.

It has always amazed me how society and the
Great forces of political and religious evil
Dupe us into believing in the Sublime and Ridiculous.
When we are young,
We are so easily influenced by forces that try so hard to turn us
into something or someone they want us to be.
What's more, they all succeed to some degree.

Depending on the nature of the political climate it can be pretty
deadly for us.
All those poor boys that were forced into fighting the Vietnam
War were permanently damaged or killed.
Nobody came out for the better.
And we never seem to count what happens to the other side.

And for what?
For some fucking ideological political bullshit agenda?
Sound familiar?

HOW DO YOU STAND UP AND "JUST SAY NO"?
I WON'T GO TO WAR NO MATTER WHAT!

The persuasive influences for god and country on us will never end.
And during certain leadership cycles they will rationalize many
perverted actions that are built on foundations of a corrupted
ideology influenced by the great financial institutions.

In the face of all the media and political pressure that can be
concocted by the government at any given moment in time,
we have to be able to

STAND UP AT ANYTIME AND SAY FUCK YOU!
YOU ARE LYING TO ME AND MY COUNTRY ONE MORE TIME

and

I'm not going along for the ride.
I will Stand Up
against all the peer pressure you can throw at me
and know that I am doing the right thing.

So how did I, Mr. Hip war resister in the '70s,
Fuck up so bad with the God and Country and President Bush
and his Iraq War?

Okay, so with all that wisdom of an old war resister that I was so
proud of my whole life to have aggressively protested back when
I was in my 20s…
How did I allow myself to get duped into believing that the Iraq
war was a worthy endeavor for our great country?

Where was I, even though I know and thought I knew better?

How could I have grown up after all these years of knowing
better and allow myself to be duped one more time?

How did my generation, who knew better, let it happen?

How did we let such a stupid bunch of thugs ruin our country
so quickly?

HOW DOES IT HAPPEN
OVER AND OVER AGAIN?

And how are we to learn the lesson so we can prevent ourselves
from being the Stupid Sheep in the March of Ideology,
Even if it is the name of Freedom.
Even in the passion of a 9/11.

IT'S MY RIDE AND I AM THE DRIVER OF MY OWN VEHICLE.

Sometimes we run out of gas and even have to hitch hike
through the South. Sometimes we even get the shit kicked out
of us because we are different.

Sometimes even though we are even stronger
than our opponent, there might be too many of them
and we are easily overwhelmed.

NOTHING IS WORSE THAN TAKING THE PAVED ROAD OF OTHER PEOPLE'S DESIGNS ON OUR OWN LIFE.

In the end, we can only feel cheated by the lack of self-expression
and

The lack of Courage in the face of knowledge that we are
unwilling to let surface, even inside our inner selves.

I am quite embarrassed that I did not see the trickery and
Sleight of hand that our country's leaders fed us.

How could I have grown so stupid?

So fucking lazy!

How do I prevent such a lack of vision again?

So you see it's not just a standard to learn something when you are young and

Know that you were right,

but you must

EXERCISE YOUR VISION TO SEE CLEARLY EVERY LIVING MOMENT.

SLACKERS ARE FOR DEAD PEOPLE.

How can I explain it to you to protect yourself when it comes down the pike again? For sure it will.

Over

And

Over

It Just Did

One More Fucking Time

Dumb

And

Dumber

There will always be another

Nixon,

Bush,

Cheney,

Trump

WHO GRAB THE POWER AND EXPLOIT THE FEAR OF THE PEOPLE TO THE DETRIMENT OF US ALL.

Fear can be such a social and political animal.

Yes we had the whole Twin Tower rational which gave us such
fodder *to*
Believe we had to react and bully somebody just to make us
Celebrate a collective feel-good revenge.
We just had to show the world we were tough.
We were led to believe that our emotions needed
to be expressed in war-like terms.
Our leaders had a different agenda.
They saw opportunity in the heat of the moment.
Who knows what it really was:
Oil
Revenge
Destiny
Democracy
Riches.
The heat of the moment can permanently change your life.
The trajectory is fragile and the
Balance can be easily distrupted.

ALWAYS BE WARY
OF THE POLITICIAN'S TONGUE.
NEVER TRUST THEM.
THE MORE OBVIOUS THEY PORTRAY
THE STORY, THE MORE RESERVATIONS
YOU HAVE TO BRING TO BEAR ON ITS
TRUTH AND RATIONALITY.

That is not to say it doesn't get complicated.

Syria

Iraq

Afghanistan

Iran

Egypt

Libya

Israel

Palestine

Angola

Somalia

Cuba…

The list will grow and grow for a long time unfortunately.

But above all

Pretend there is draft at all times and that you or your son and daughter may be the one who has to give a

Life

Arm

Leg

Dreams

For a far off country and for a reason that you have no fucking idea what and why.

POLITICALLY STAY A SKEPTIC TILL THE DAY YOU DIE.
NO MATTER HOW OLD
STAY AWARE AND ACTIVE WITH
THE POWER OF YOUTH IN YOUR HEART
AND VOTE IN <u>EVERY</u> ELECTION!

I HAD THE GREAT FORTUNE
TO RANDOMLY WALK OVER TO THE
LIBRARY OF CONGRESS,
my favorite building in
Washington D.C., and to my surprise
Noel Paul Stookey,
of Peter, Paul and Mary, and
Ramblin Jack Elliot were
performing and celebrating
the 100th anniversary of
Woody Guthrie.

IN 1970 AND 1971, NOEL AND I HAD NUMEROUS ENCOUNTERS,

as I was one of the go-to concert organizers from D.C.
to Boston for the anti-war movement, and Noel
and his musical mate Peter Yarrow were always the first
to commit to many important concerts and protests,
which in the end contributed significantly to the social tipping
point to end the Vietnam War.

In that time of my youth,
Music for social change was
Bound in the Glory of a
More ethical union,

NOT A MORE PERFECT UNION, BUT A MORE ETHICAL ONE.

The one pervasive ideology that we held strong was that
Not only were we changing the world, but
We also had a long-term vision that
Turning on would create
A more ethical person, who would
Affect all those around us.

We believed if everybody got high, and eventually those who were straight just died off, we would have succeeded in a new world order, at least in our country.

The forces of the financial establishment are very strong.

I AM NOT EXACTLY SURE WHEN AND HOW IT HAPPENED, BUT MY GENERATION FAILED AND DID SO MISERABLY.

Sitting in the venerable Library of Congress,
I asked during the question and answer:
What would Woody have done today during an election season
of partisan madness?
How would Woody have organized the apathetic youth of today
To stand up for the precious right to vote
The universal right for health care for the poor and uninsured
Marriage equality?

Would Woody have been more successful to
Wake up the sleeping youth who still
Are not conscious of the direct results for
Not showing up to vote in every election?

ELECTIONS HAVE CONSEQUENCES

Unfortunately, we just saw that Pie in the Face

Imagine if the intensity of the early 1970s and
Our core ethical and social standards that we fought for with
national unity Were never given up?

We replaced that passion and belief protocol with our
Selfish, wealth-seeking independence and
Disregard for a more perfect world
built on compassion for all.

Ironically, the energy transference on a social basis from
the "ethical pot high" to the "hard-drug coke high" stimulated
the downfall.

Maybe our generation,
Asleep at the wheel, were
So morally and ethically lazy
To allow two wars to go on for a decade just
Because there was no draft and
Our own kids were never in the crossfire.

Here's the shit:

WHEN WE ARE YOUNG, WE KNOW THAT YOUTH, WITH ITS BOUNDLESS ENERGY HAS SUCH A MONUMENTAL ABILITY TO AFFECT AND INFLUENCE SOCIAL WAVES.

How do we protect that power source as we grow families and jobs and businesses that have this strange way of marginalizing the very essence of everything we stood for?

Front and Center?

How is it when we are young, we naturally distrust political power messaging? Yet we get corrupted so easily in our 30s, 40s, and 50s,

Only to wake up in our 60s,

Realizing we fucked up along the way, and

Got over our heads

And embraced

And Nurtured a

National Political and a Social platform that

Lacks the social compassions that were

The Core meaning of our life in our 20s.

Here's my take:

Holding onto the magical power of Social Justice and Ethical Democracy and Support for Political Compassion for

The Truths that we find Self Evident in Youth is like

Going to the Gym.

THE OLDER WE GET, THE MORE IMPORTANT IS EXERCISE AND THE GYM

The same goes for a continued
Commitment to the values that
Supported our youthful enterprises.

Change may have the appearance it is happening naturally
and in an unusually fast time frame with the connectivity and
social power of the Internet, but with a quick slight of hand,
The wrong boneheads in government can reverse social
progress way too quickly.

This is not a party issue of D's versus R's.

POLITICAL AND SOCIAL ACTIVISM IS A LIFELONG COMMITMENT AND IT'S NEVER OVER.
FUCKING <u>NEVER!</u>

AND IT STARTS THE MOMENT YOU WAKE UP

The Toothpaste you use
The Coffee and Tea
The Water
The Car

It's easy to get a fat belly after 40 years old.

I guess it's easier to go to war

If the grown ups are not watching the shop and

Don't give a fuck how much it can ruin society.

The Millennials will get their own turn at events.

Now For Sure.

It is Upon Us Once Again.

HISTORY REPEATS IN STRANGE WAYS

And there may not be

Enough Woodys or

Bonos or

Bruces

To Wake you up out of your Dream

Or

Nightmare

If you have been sleeping for too long.

Beware of the Bush in the Forest!

BEWARE OF THE LIES
KNOWLEDGE AND TRUTH
ARE MISSION CRITICAL

I can say deeply and regrettably that I am convinced that my generation lost its way.

My generation's past social failure cannot be reversed but the future can be.

Where does technology and democracy fit into this platform?

INEVITABLY, TECHNOLOGY WILL LEVEL ALL PLAYING FIELDS

and

Soon enough

One Man,

One Woman,

One Vote will

Deliver the Democratic Power and equalization that our founding fathers originally envisioned for our country.

The application of technology in democracy is why this generation of youth will be more powerful than anyone before it. However, this is why your engagement and commitment to a lifetime focus on the ethics in democracy and compassion in the political process (whatever your personal political persuasion) will have a new and enhanced meaning in society.

THE FRUITS OF A CONNECTED DEMOCRACY WILL ENABLE A PURER STATE OF REPRESENTATIVE GOVERNMENT.

A Connected Nation where we All count, not only our Vote in an election, but one with an ongoing presence of position in the process of Legislation.

► ## LEGISLATION IS WHAT REALLY CHANGES OUR LIVES.

► ## THE SUPREME COURT CAN ELECT A PRESIDENT

► ## ULTIMATELY WITH A CONNECTED DEMOCRACY, IN THE END, PLURALITY WILL WIN.
YOUR VOTE COUNTS AND IT STARTS WITH EVERY BREATH YOU TAKE.

WHEN YOU WAKE UP AND
WHEN YOU LIE DOWN.
Remember that the best time
to take that realistic personal inventory
is in the beginning of the day.
Everything is always clearer
in the beginning.

RECENTLY, I HAVE BEEN STRUGGLING

whether or not to make an important deal with my company
and yesterday I made my list of the pros and cons of the deal.
The pros seemed to completely outweigh the cons. I went to bed
convincing myself that it was OK to go along with this deal.

When I awoke this morning, my first thought was that
I had missed the most important reason not to do the deal.
My early morning clarity allowed me to see the original
long-term reason why we had started our company
in the first place.

POINT:
► FRESHNESS OF THE EARLY MIND
AND CLARITY OF THOUGHTS WHEN
WE FIRST AWAKE ARE CRUCIAL FOR
SUCCESS
HEALTH AND

WEALTH.

Don't tell me you love me because

I don't want to know.

I care how you act.

I care how you eat.

I care how you work.

I care how you dress,

I care how you keep your nails,

I care how you talk and

What you talk about.

IT'S THE ACTIONS THAT MATTER.
MOMENT TO MOMENT.
EDIT TO EDIT.
FRAME TO FRAME.

The creative goal of self-realization lies in the

Center of the frame of life.

It is there that all the set decoration, training, and learning

must go on.

The healthy rejuvenation of

The primary cells of our being has to be the

Basic quest at center stage.

This involves a total surrender to the spiritual element
That the single cell represents the whole.

WITHIN THE SINGLE CELL ARE ALL THE SECRETS OF THE UNIVERSE.

SO FOCUS ON YOURSELF AND GO AS DEEP AS YOU CAN AND GET IN TOUCH WITH YOUR OWN SINGLE CELL.

Start there and don't worry about building anything beyond,
Only Within It.

ONCE YOU IDENTIFY
THE PRIMARY ELEMENTS OF
THE ESSENCE THAT IS YOUR SEED
OR CELL YOU CAN
FREE YOURSELF THROUGH
INNER PERSONAL KNOWLEDGE
INNER PERSONAL CONNECTIVITY
INNER PERSONAL CONSCIOUSNESS.

Essentially we are machines that form the framed work or
Foundation for our single cells to marry and
Reproduce themselves.
Healthy fusion breathes life to the flower of the cell.

LEARN TO LOOK INSIDE
AND IDENTIFY **YOUR ELEMENTS.**
ENGAGE YOUR ELEMENTS.

The comfort, warmth, and growth that is generated from
the process is very Healthy and

Breeds

Good life.

Good life equals:

Good marriage,

Good family,

Good security,

Good product,

Good person,

Good Father

Good Mother.

Good Son

Good Daughter

All of which Breeds

Good Health

Tangible Wealth

Spiritual Success.

THE INTERNET HAS TRANSFORMED US ALL BY ITS DEMOCRATIC PLATFORM OF THE INDIVIDUAL, accelerating the evolution of our society and culture to a degree that will forever change the fabric of our personal universe.

THE INTERNET IS THE CHRIST CHILD.
MOSES.
THE MESSIAH.
THE COVENANT OF THE ARCHANGELS.

The essence of the godhead in all religions is that there is a
Universal connectivity to the
Magic and
Source of a soul's energy field.

Just like the mysteries of the DNA,
The computer chip can be just as supernatural.

Can the power and unfathomable expression that the entire
Human universe can finally
Connect Itself to Itself
Be any less godly than some of the scriptures written
In a far off foreign language about parting seas and plagues?

Can a tiny speck of sand turned into a silicon chip with
Endless boundaries and energy be
Any less powerful than a molecule of blood carrying
the history of life in its DNA?

What about the history of life in that grain of sand?
Are we all not that grain of sand in the end,
One and the Same?

IF LIFE IS BUT A REFLECTION OF THE SOUL IN EVERY EXISTENCE? IS NOT THE INTERNET FAMILY OF MANKIND?

The Quantum science of the Kabbalah shows us that our life
existence can be as confounding from the
Great distance of space as it is
Spatial nothingness under the electron microscope.

THIS IS WHY I ADHERE TO THE **PERSONAL SCIENCE OF THE PROCESS** OF THE DAY POWER AND WHY THE **PROCESS IS THE EMBODIMENT OF FULFILLMENT.**

Happiness,

Success and the

Evolution of our spirit can only be achieved

Moment by Moment through the

Process of the work ethic and

Daily habits in its minutia execution of the detail that

Comprise the sum total of a day's experience.

Therein lies the path to

True happiness and

Fulfillment.

Therein lies the

Daily Seeds of Immortality.

BORN INTO OLD SCHOOL JEW LAND.
Hardwired by My Father
Shabbat was Holy and Special
Kosher was Unconditional
Marry a Jew was Unconditional

I was Lucky
I had No Choice

ONE DAY I BROUGHT MY GIRLFRIEND HOME AND DAD REALLY DIDN'T WANT TO LET HER IN THE HOUSE.

She was a blonde trust-fund baby.
I loved her but knew inside I could never marry her
and be fulfilled as a family unit.

Not Really A Question of Fulfillment

I am sure I could have had a marriage of sincere love
and companionship. She was a trooper and in those daze we
were crazy into the '70s culture of Drugs and Rock and Roll.
My partner had to be able to fly over the edge of security
and still hold a strong and steady hand of courage.

Fulfillment had to do with Family and Father.

Being Hard Wired, I didn't think I would have been able to
have normal relations with her and My Father. Isadore was an
overbearing and towering figure. He carried his Jewishness in
every step. Not like we were forced to comply with the rituals
and culture.

It was His Way or the Highway.

When I introduced my first wife-to-be to Dad, Stella, who was Moroccan–an Arab–Dad did not really trust if she was Jewish. He asked her to read the Friday night Kiddush prayer. She put Dad to rest by telling him she was the daughter of Esther and a long line of rabbis, and that she was well versed in the oral teachings of Kabbalah.

All along my life road, I have always found comfort in the Sounds of Prayers and the Spirit of Religion.

WITH RELIGION, WHAT MATTERS IS TO LET IT RESONATE INSIDE YOUR SOUL. ALL RELIGIONS SPEAK THE SAME LANGUAGE IN THEIR PURE STATE. I KNOW WE WANDER IN AND OUT OF THE RITUALS BUT THE CULTURE OF WHO WE ARE NEVER GOES AWAY

Being the youngest of an older generation, I have been able to enjoy a transformative journey from Orthodox Judaism to the spiritual road of Buddhism.

In my second life I married, Laurie, a Jew-Bhu, and
Even though I supported and joined her often in many
Buddhist rituals and travelled to Tibet and Bhutan,
I never could Release
The Throngs of My Father's Religion.

One God
No Image
No Son of God
No Deity to Transform
No Real After Life

At a special retreat with Gelek Rimpoche,
I finally stripped away the Jewish chains and allowed myself
to experience the Power and Beauty of Buddhism.
I still have trouble embracing the transformative process
of using images of Buddha or Tara or any of the deities as
forms of meditative pathways. However, at this retreat,
I finally allowed my spirit to accept that there are
Multiple Pathways to Enlightenment.

Jesus may be the Son of God
Abraham the Father of the Jews
Mohammed the Messenger of God

Buddha is just another Holy Pathway through which we all may
ride higher in our evolution and deeper to
Find the Meaning of Life.

However, the conflicts of our religion from birth continue to
collide with our love partnerships our whole life.
Our relationships with the Holy Fathers and Fathers never quite
work themselves out.

It's a long Journey.

AS KIDS, MANY OF US ARE ALLERGIC TO GOD.

I fought my religion and am constantly reminded by my siblings
how much I drove my father crazy.
Life repeats itself in many ways through our kids.
I think it's easy to get allergic because so much of the trappings
of religion are archaic and convoluted.

WE CONFUSE RELIGION AND RITUAL WITH GOD.

We confuse the Archetypal Figures with the Message.

I watched the Pope in Madison Square Garden and
I love Pope Francis.
I love and embrace his message.
Yet I have trouble relating to the image of Jesus on a cross.
I understand how easy it is to reject and be allergic.

Yet I do believe that the birth of any sentient being proves the
existence of God.
And that
We Do Not have to Define God.

IT'S OK NOT TO BELIEVE IN GOD.

What is important to know is that

WE ARE OUR GOD AND
GOD IS ETERNAL AND LIVES INSIDE US.

And that
We Are Eternal.

Be careful not to become too allergic to our inner soul and spirit where God lives.

And do not confuse
God and Religion
God and Tradition
God and Culture

TRADITION IS AN IMPORTANT FOUNDATION OF IDENTITY. IDENTITY KEEPS US ALIVE AND HEALTHY.

A Healthy and Honest Identity
Breeds Security.

Our Seeds Before Us
And After Us
Benefit from a Pure Identity
Inside
And Out

I understand the old school belief of marrying a partner from our same religion and I accept that as valid in the school of traditional protection of family and culture. Yet as parents today, we are overtaken with intermarriage and the erosion of the cultural, ritual, and religious structures that our parents and their parents fought for and
Lost their Lives over for Generations.

What Wins
What Triumphs
Is
The Ethics and Moral Base that a Partner brings to the Union
of Marriage
Together
Supported in a United Vision
Of Who We Are
Where We Came From
Who We Came From
And
That Foundation of Love Of the Whole Family Unit
Is the Center of Love.

We are All Hard Wired
One Way or Another
Breaking With Respect is a Dignified Process

The DNA will be there, but I believe that DNA is enhanced
and enriched by ritual and cultural practice. I respect the right
of self-determination as a basic foundation of life and one that
promotes health and self-wealth of spirit.

In the face of intermarriage, I believe that maintaining and
continuing to embrace Our Historical Identity,
no matter how diminished it may have become in youth,
is vital to a healthy, long-term relationship
with our partners and our kids
And supports our Long-Term Spiritual Journey.

It's crucial to Open Ourselves to
Explore and Immerse Multiple Spiritual Pathways.

There is One God
That One God is Inside Us
Not Outside.
There are Many Pathways
Many Roads
They will Change Over Time.

WHAT DOES NOT CHANGE IS
WHERE WE CAME FROM
WHO WE ARE WHEN WE STARTED
WHERE ARE PARENTS STARTED

Youth carries a natural state of rebellion, which starts as soon
as we get off our Mommy's Milk.
We have to be careful to be able to nurture and control that
rebellion as we enter our adult years.

It's important to
REBEL AGAINST OUR TEACHERS,
REBEL AGAINST OUR RELIGION.
REBEL AGAINST OUR PARENTS

Beware when the rebellion enters inside
and against our Inner Child.
That is where conflict starts to break down the positive effects
of self-growth. In the end, if we go too far,
we find ourselves alone within ourselves.

That's The Precious Identity of Who We Are

WHERE WE COME FROM
WHO OUR PARENTS ARE
WHERE OUR PARENTS CAME FROM
NEVER GOES AWAY
WE CAN REBEL AGAINST ALL
WE CANNOT WASH AWAY OUR IDENTITY.

IT IS OUR DNA.

So yes,
Run Hard in Any Direction.
Love and Embrace your partner from any religion or culture
no matter how difficult family relations may be.

NEVER LOSE SIGHT AND LOVE OF
HOW OF THE STRUCTURAL CHILD
CAME INTO THIS WORLD WITH
THE LONG TAIL ROOTS OF OUR DNA.

AND GIVE YOUR CHILDREN THAT GIFT

IT'S TOO EASY TO LEAVE IT BEHIND.

MY WHOLE ADULT LIFE I WAS AN INDEPENDENT PRODUCER, DIRECTOR, AND DISTRIBUTOR OF ENTERTAINMENT. My life was a long series of ups and downs with the constant need to have numerous projects percolating all the time to ensure that at least one of them would produce the needed cash flow to sustain life and family.

WHEN YOU WORK IN INDEPENDENT FILM AND TV YOU AUTOMATICALLY HAVE VARIETY BECAUSE EACH PROJECT IS DIFFERENT.

One of the most compelling aspects of entertainment production is that shit changes all the time, and the subject matter of the projects usually bring varied rewards with a freshness of creativity.

Of course, that reward is easily offset by the stress and uncertainty of never really knowing what the fuck the outcome will be of the production.

I think much of both my fascination and attraction to entertainment production was based on the newness of every project.

During the Go Go days of *Night Flight* in the 1980s, I remember having to fire many employees and how I developed a sincere belief that I was doing every person I fired I good deed.

We were all young and there was plenty of opportunity, so it wasn't like I was robbing families of livelihood. In my heart I knew that I would be forcing them to start over again and that would be healthy in the long run for them.

I used to take them out for lunch, get both of us buzzed,
and then give them the "this is good for you" speech.
Buzzed in those daze was usually a two martini lunch!

Then the Internet came along and change took a whole new
meaning for everyone!
In the Old Daze
Change was something that was a painful and
slow personal platform.
It was easy to fear and full of all sorts of unknowns that scared
the shit out of us.

The Internet has made change a culture full of excitement
and anticipation about waking up the next day, because
we know anything can happen quickly and without prior notice.
Now, The Next Big Thing is happening with ease
and out of nowhere on a daily basis.

I can still remember getting my first color TV.
Imagine that you will tell your kids when they are in their 40s,
that you remember when Facebook and Google first burst
on the scene, just like we laugh about the fax or answering
machines of my generation.

Who knows, they might not even know what Facebook is
in 40 years.

SO WHAT'S THE BIG
DEAL ABOUT CHANGE?
IF THE INTERNET IS
ALREADY FORCING A
CHANGING CULTURE,
WHY IS THERE
A PERSONAL NEED
TO CHANGE AND
WHY IS IT HEALTHY?

Simply, doing the same job or
Producing the same content over and over
Every day makes us boring inside to ourselves and therefore
Boring to our friends and loved ones around us.

The other side of the coin asks:
How do we temper the ideal of perfecting ourselves in our
profession and not get bored when forced by the
Pursuit of Perfection that Necessitates Repetition?

I believe one of the answers is:
Prepare yourself to hang on, not necessarily to your job,
But your profession and
Your professional skill set.

A fundamental strategy is to
Never Be Afraid of Getting Fired!
We have to be able to stand up to our boss or partner
Without Fear.

I realize that Creative Courage has its own
Hunger for New Frontiers.

It's so easy to succumb to daily habits in our jobs without
challenging ourselves.
We get so scared when we are working on new ground
as it heightens the fear of failure or mistakes.

I have found that Breaking New Creative Ground is the
Most Rewarding of All
Even with all the Fear and Loathing that comes with it.

In the End
It's all about
The Learn.
Learn.
Learn.

TO LEARN SOMETHING NEW EVERY DAY
IS A QUEST FOR LIFE
UNTIL YOUR LAST DYING BREATH.

Have to be Able to
Jump Off the Cliff
and
Fly
or
Die A Boring Life.
Unsatisfied
Unfulfilled
Believe in Your Potential
Never Stop Reaching for It
Learn Something New Every Day.

I JUST FINISHED WATCHING THE GAMBLER
AND LOVED THE MORAL OF THE STORY:
GET TO THE POINT
TO BE ABLE TO SAY FUCK YOU:

Fuck You to your Boss
Fuck You to your Bankers
Fuck You to your Parents
Fuck You to your Wife
Fuck You to your Husband
Fuck You to your Children
Fuck You to Yourself

Buy a house as soon in life that you can muster the 20% deposit. Only buy what a 15-year mortgage can support.

If you are in your 30s and have saved $50,000, you can buy a house or apartment for $250,000.
A 15-year mortgage will be paid off by the time you are 50, and then you can live for the next 50 years without the stress of a mortgage.

I know the flaw in this concept is that we are now a moving generation.

Who wants to commit to a 15-year mortgage in the same city? It's Sooo Inflexible.

ALL I CAN SAY IS TIME FLIES AND IT'S A DECADE JUST TO START TO GET GOOD AT ANYTHING.
THINK LONG
LIFE IS LONG

.

AND GETTING LONGER.

WITHOUT THE ABILITY TO BE ABLE TO SAY FUCK YOU. CHANCES ARE YOU WILL BE STRESSED YOUR WHOLE LIFE.

We are Bamboo
We do not Break in the Winds of Change
For Mid-Life to Fully Blossom
We need the financial support of a sound and
whole life family plan that
Includes the Quest for an Interest-Free Life.

I have lived successfully and unsuccessfully
above my means most of my life.
It has been a nonstop Juggling Act.
I always felt that money didn't matter that much (Fuck you)
That my freedom was derived from
My Happy Go Lucky Spiritual Foundation.
It started as a child born with a Silver Spoon
As my Mom always told me.
Now at 69, I realize I should have been so much more aware that
we could create a stronger base of personal freedom by starting
to save in the beginning on your first job.

START YOUNG TO MAKE LONG-TERM INVESTMENTS.
THE FUTURE COMES WAY TOO FAST.

Dad always said
"Make more at 10%, sleep better at 5%."

It's hard to think long when we are young.
It's a vision that needs cultivation.
Credit cards suck.
They are the Cocaine of the Banks.
They are the hammer in the capitalist system and
We are the nails that get driven deeper and deeper.

I can't count the times that one of
my credit card limits was raised
Only to find myself again at its higher limit.

Train the Long Vision and
Create a Self Identity of
What You Want to Be in 20 Years.
And believe that you can live to 100 in good health.

It's amazing how much financial security can be achieved
in two decades.

Ten years ago, I hired a laborer on the ferry for $10 an hour.
He didn't even have a bike. He always showed up on time.
He was always polite and positive.
We gave him one of our good extra bikes.
He worked hard, was responsible and dependable.

Now, 10 years later,
He told me that he saved $100,000 and bought a nice farm
in his native country.
He never had a credit card!

My kid, Dorian, for Father's Day, told me that the best gift I
gave him was no college debt so that he was able to tell his boss
anything without fear that he may lose his job.

I am Old School

I believe that parents should go broke to support their children's college education.

FUCK YOU
IS A STATE OF MIND

A State of Bamboo

A State of No Credit Card Debt

A State of No Mortgage

A State of Honesty

A State of Transparency

A State of Love

Love of Ourselves,

Love of our Loved Ones,

Love of our Future

Love of our Life.

Love of our Freedom

Love of Money in the Bank

Love of Cash!

And Start Your 401K

On Your First Job

On Your First Day of Work!

I GREW UP THE SON OF A JUNK MAN, ISADORE SHAPIRO, THE SON OF ABRAHAM SHAPIRO, AN IMMIGRANT JEW FROM RUSSIA. As family lore goes, Abraham had the cart and his brother Samuel had the horse. They both started as street peddlers. Samuel's family became the car dealers and Abraham the junk man.

Like my brother Ed and my cousin Jamie, my cousin Artie and
I peddled junk every summer through high school and college.
We learned the art, which was bonded in our DNA, to see that
scrap had its value, and to collect it and sell it to my Dad
was a wonderful game.

Buy Low,
Lift Strong,
And produce a
High Profit Margin
From Shit Someone is Always Willing to Throw Away.

This Lifelong Lesson gave me the Basis of my Creative Cutting
Edge Stability.

THERE IS ALWAYS VALUE IN THE STREETS.

It's not just about plastic bottles, and yes, I did go around with
my red wagon cart and pick up newspapers.

In the street is in your eye!
In your eye is all around you.
Everything you see, feel, touch, and think you're going to see next.
Everything you think you already forget.

Everything you already had a thought of, but can't remember even a second after you glimmered that genius thought.

The strength that we can derive from a natural belief in our own creativity can be nurtured in the fact that all around us we are surrounded by assets of free content, within which anything is possible to build our next dream into reality.

In the Creative and Producing business, many times we tend to inhibit ourselves because we don't think we can obtain rights to an idea but remember:

Original ideas are free!

THE INTERNET IS THE ULTIMATE JUNK YARD OF ENDLESS OPPORTUNITIES.

The Library of Congress is full of millions of free-content opportunities.

Public domain copyrights, products, and music provide an amazing wealth to tap forever.

The point here is to never be afraid of the unknown.
Trust there is free junk in your own yard of endless opportunities, filled with endless assets to build your dreams.

Rest assured, we can find security in the fact that one Man's Junk is another Man's Dreams.

Be bold and know that creative ideas for the brave are never ending.

COURAGE IS A FLOWER WE ALL HAVE GROWING INSIDE OURSELVES.

Never be afraid of getting fired.

Never go to work afraid to express yourself boldly.

We often think the consequences of bold self-expression may produce negative results streaming from the fear of ending up on the Junk Yard Street.

The real negative is living in the Valley of the Walking Dead *because* We are Afraid of Consequence.

FUCK YOUR BOSS.
BE STRONG.
BELIEVE IN YOUR SELF.

Believe there is always a better job.

Jump off the Cliff if you are unhappy with your current platform.

We can all Fly if We Believe We Can Fly.

After all we Do Fly in Dreams, Don't We?

I GREW UP IN A WEALTHY,
SMALL-TOWN FAMILY.
My father, a junk man, always had
cash in his pocket and tons of copper
and other valuable metals in his
warehouse. I had the innate sense
of security built into my DNA as
I knew I could always figure out
how to make a living.
I knew there was always money
in the street.

WHAT I DIDN'T REALIZE WAS THAT SECURITY WAS MY BLIND EYE.

I was an independent entrepreneur and rocketeer my whole life and
Much of it I lived above my means.

My sister always asked me if I was "socking away some money"
and I always had some excuse or acerbic response.

I would prefer to jump on a plane and travel business class
to a foreign country rather then
Count My Pennies and
Save for a Rainy Day.

Good News-Bad News
The Rainy Days Really Came.
The Struggle Never Ended.
The Creative Process Always had Fertile Ground

In the '70s and '80s I probably spent more money on drugs than
was measurable.
I could have bought a building or two or a piece of land at the
beach for
Just one year's worth of Partying Drugs.

Looking back, it's hard imagining how I could have seen through
the daze of youth into a different platform of future security.

It's so fucking hard to break the ignorance of youthful exuberance.
That sense that we are immortal and all will be OK
even if we tempt the winds of fate over and over.

The problem is that youth disappears really quickly and the
The Forces of Age Never Stop once we turn down that road.

I am not even suggesting to lose the spirit of youth, as that is
The Main Source of Light in all our Creative Lives.

I am suggesting that saving a penny a day in the beginning
of life and treating your pennies as capital to never lose is
A Habit as Important as Brushing Your Teeth.

My friend Jon Says:
"Only Floss the Teeth You Want to Keep."

It's All about the Habits!
Habits are Key to Success
Or
Failure

Do you stop and bend down to pick up a penny in the street or is it
Too worthless for the act?

I think we have all walked by that penny more than once.

Every time I don't stop I have this strange feeling inside me that I am fucked up.

In the age of zero interest rates, we are instilled with a false sense that money has limited value because it is not earning anything.

When I was Young,
Money for Nothing,
I want my MTV.
Money for drugs gave us a party high worth no lasting value.

I believe that conundrum drove a senseless value about money as an asset to cherish.

Today, even our precious iPhones become worthless after two years.

I am still using my father's orange juicer 60 years later.

Can't imagine my son would use any new machine of 2017 in 60 years.
The juicer will probably work if there is still electricity around!

So how do we build and protect and cherish and maintain our capital assets?

What would be a capital asset if there were world calamities and banks failed?

At some point in our lives we transform from an individual state to one of our family.
And then our family grows up and

We transform back to a more individual state generally between our wife, husband, or partner,
While our children grow their own families.

In the old days, families, even though they sprouted off,
There was always a continued responsibility to the extended family.

Today it's harder to maintain the bonds with our children and their families, as resettling at long distances breaks intimacy.
Sometimes I wonder how I would walk from New York to L.A. to find my son
If there was no transportation and
How far would I go to support him in a time of need?

The answer is
As Far and as Long as Necessary.
and
On My Knees if Needed.

If I knew he had his piece of land with fresh water and the ability to grow food, I would be much more secure than if his apartment on the 13th floor no longer had running water and electricity.

So yes,
Sock it away like Brushing your Teeth.
Protect the cash.
Nurture the Asset.

Today I am in the high country in the middle of Italy.
We walked up the street and Pasquolo and Delfina served us a glass of white wine from their own land and figs from their 40-year-old tree.

Life really can be simple
A 40-year-old fig tree is a Real Asset.

A pear tree is for the heirs.

Next door a winery is using a 250-year barrel to store their wine.
It was always in the family.

That's a Capital Asset!

DAD WAS AN OLD SCHOOL YET
SOPHISTICATED BUSINESS MAN,
he believed in the purity of his word
and that honesty in business
and personal life was a foundational
element to life.

ONE OF DAD'S LASTING LESSONS WAS THE IMPORTANCE OF GOING OUT OF YOUR WAY TO MEET FACE-TO-FACE WITH CLIENTS.

He used to take me on trips to the great paper mills along the rivers in Massachusetts. One of them was the famous Crane Paper, which produced the paper for dollar bills. Dad was always proud as a Ragman that every dollar bill had some of his pure white, 100 percent cotton rags in them. He always emphasized that his cotton had to be pure and that even the smallest impurity would ruin an entire shipment.

This interwoven lesson is that relationships in business are personal and need the personal interaction to thrive. If you carry honesty in your persona as a natural state of your presence, that will enhance the value of personal relationships. And more importantly, it will attract more clearly and naturally targeted those individuals who share your values.

I took this to heart and have carried these fundamental lessons with me my whole life.

In today's connected world, there is a greater tendency to live online and go years without ever even meeting some of your main clients. And both of you think this is absolutely acceptable. It's not that you can't flourish with an online or telephone relationship, it's just that face-to-face relationships always fare better and will produce more Long Lasting Successful Results and Stronger Relationships.

And Google Hangouts and FaceTime don't count.

There is another important aspect to this, and that is Building Respect.

I have found that going out of my way to meet clients, associates, friends, and family generates a different degree of warmth, understanding, and closeness.

People truly do respect you more when you drag your ass and go out of your way to meet them.

The farther you travel and the more aggravation you go through will always generate much more positive energy and respect on both sides of the relationship.

When it comes to family, we have to be even more vigilant to maintain the personal touch. Most of us will move far away from our families, brothers, sisters, cousins, aunts, and uncles, but once we have kids it is even more important to go out of our way to keep the personal contact going. It's a pain in the ass to fly back across the country for graduations and special occasions, but The Rewards are so valuable, they are those Special Gifts that Keep on Giving.

IF YOU THINK YOU ARE GOING TO BE SORRY THAT YOU MISSED AN EVENT, DON'T MISS IT! **ALWAYS ERR ON THE SIDE OF GOING.**

AT MY 50TH BIRTHDAY PARTY,
I came to realize that friends who
I had known for 20 years or longer
were the foundation of my security
as a connected individual
amongst an extended family.
We tend to focus on our bloodlines,
but fail to fully support and
believe in the inner strength of our
connected tribe in the bigger picture.

A COLLEGE ROOMMATE FRIENDSHIP AND LOVE WILL LAST AS STRONG AS EVER.

What keeps it alive?

How do we keep those old special friendships delivering new fruit as we grow?

How do we nurture the organic health of friendship in the face of commercial expressions of friendships that are seemingly more important in the short run because of our careers?

My best friend Philip and I became really good friends when I had moved to Austin for a brief interlude in my career. Upon leaving and moving back to L.A., we agreed that in order to maintain our important friendship we needed to institute a code of a weekly Shabbat telephone call. That was almost 20 years ago. What has transpired is that we have these weekly calls during which we share our week's accomplishments and goals, some of which we achieved and others we are still trying to catch. But the intimacy and beauty of the friendship has far surpassed what would have evolved if we had just kept in touch once in a while.

The same has held for my eight college roommates and fraternity brothers. Every year we try to get together and spend a long weekend just hanging together, getting high like the old daze, and basking in the love of lifelong friendships. And every year it becomes more and more precious.

HERE'S THE SECRET:
- ► FRIENDSHIPS TAKE COMMITMENT.
- ► COMMITMENTS TAKE DISCIPLINE.
- ► THE ART IS TO COMMIT TO GUARANTEED COMMUNICATION OF INTIMATE CONTACTS.

When Philip and I talk, we share, and because we share on a regular basis, we have become intimate in our struggles to grow and learn and get a tiny bit closer to enlightened understanding of ourselves.

We also care about what the other person has done for the week and is planning to do, because we take the time to listen and share without any agenda.

Neither of us needs anything but love and the willingness to share
To make our love and friendship return
That Special Fruit of Life that Grows with Real Friends.

I am not sure, in the new age of Social Media, how the 20-year club will affect intimacy of primary friends. I suspect that the tendency will be to forgo the touch and getting together because of increased ability to be friended on Facebook.

My recommendation is to protect those special friends by committing to in-person relationships and old fashion telephone conversations without a time limit.

THERE IS ALSO ANOTHER 20-YEAR CLUB: COLLECTING AND INVESTING.

Hold on to that piece of art or apartment and think
only in decades.
What could I have, would have, should have bought 20 years ago
that would have created financial freedom 20 years later,
If I had the Vision
The passion
The tenacity
The luck to hold on to what became the Warhol, the Keith Haring,
the shack on the beach,
The piece of Land with Water?

What can we buy today that will graduate with honors in 20 years and how do we generate that Vision?

High resolution is one determining factor.
Uniqueness.
A single painting by a master is a unique work of art.
Single in the universe.
Immortality as an object of Life and Creativity.

Concentrate on uniqueness and singularity.
Collect original over limited editions and lithographs.

A photograph from negative film will in time be of much greater value than digital works of art.

I have a theory that there will be an awakening in 20 years, that more than a decade's of digital art will be lost in hard drives and flash cards, while the original art and photos from film and more organics will overtake the digital universe in accelerated value.

There won't be that many 1966 GTO convertibles left in 2040. Can you imagine how beautiful and rare chrome bumpers will look in 20 years?
Of course there may not be any fuel to run them…but that is another story.

High Resolution:

Newspapers Fade.

Protect your paper.

Life will be cheaper. But luxury will be more expensive.

Plan luxury in 20-year investments.

We don't get rich and suddenly get luxury.

Luxury is something we acquire through

The Expression of Joy in Every Day of Life.

DEFINE WHAT LUXURY IS TO YOU, AND TARGET IT WITH A CONSERVATIVE, NEVER-ENDING FOCUS AND VISION.

Luxury is not a Material Essence

Luxury is the Feeling Inside we Derive from

The Material and Spiritual Contact

With Ourselves and Others.

AS A TEENAGER, THE ONLY CAREER
I THOUGHT I EVER WANTED WAS
TO BE A SELF-STYLED PROMOTER
IN THE MUSIC BUSINESS.
I was pretty lucky because growing up,
I spent the summer months in the
Berkshires and worked as an usher
at both Tanglewood and the
Berkshire Music Barn.

The Berkshire Music Barn was totally unique, as it was the summer residence of the Modern Jazz Quartet and Dave Brubeck played there regularly. So when the Berkshire Music Barn went out of business while I was in college, I became obsessed with reviving it with a new and larger outdoor stage.

In my senior year, in between protesting the Vietnam War and graduating, I prepared the concert series, built a new stage, and launched the beginning of a decade of rock and folk concerts.

WELL, DREAMS CAN COME TRUE, BUT THAT DOESN'T MEAN YOU FIT IN THEM VERY EASILY ONCE THEY HAVE SPROUTED AROUND YOU.

My first concert was with hometown hero Arlo Guthrie, and it was great success. However, for the next several days the rain came and never seemed to stop. Success quickly washed into, "What the fuck am I going to do now?"

My true realization came the night of the Ike and Tina Turner concert. As it turned out, it rained the day before and up until just before the concert, and few people showed up for the show. So after a short set of 30 minutes, Ike and Tina cut the show short and walked off the stage. Normally, a band received 50% of the fee up front in advance, and the remainder after the show performance.

So here I was with my big brother Ed, who was in his early stages of being a lawyer, and he is holding this check in his hand waving it front of Ike, boldly pronouncing he was not going to pay him for a short set.

In a split second, Ike pulls a switchblade and grabs the check right out of my brother's hand and declares: "What the fuck are going to do now mother fucker!"

At that very moment, this 22-year-old kid from North Adams has the self-realization that he is out of his league and in the wrong business.

It happened one other time a few years later. I started a new kind of concert production company with a friend who had a lot of experience in producing outdoor shows. It was called *Rock and Road*. The concept was to produce rock concerts and Formula races at the same time, in the same venue. Our first major event was the Road Atlanta Grand Prix featuring the Atlanta Rhythm Section as the headliner band and a Formula 5000 race that featured Mario Andretti. Just hours before the gates opened, the representative from one of the local social clubs came into our office and announced that they were operating the box office and collecting the live gate receipts, not our staff, and that this was customary at this venue.

Of course I knew this was a stick up. I was freaking out, and I will never forget, this guy comes right up close to my face and says: "Do you think for a second a Jew from New York is going to come down here to Atlanta and My race track and run things the way you want, and collect our money from our people…no fucking way Jew Boy."

Dreams have their complications… I made two career decisions after Road Atlanta: One was I had to be in a business where Jews were accepted. The second one was to work in a field that was still successful when it rained.

I knew I had heavy Rain Karma every time I produced an event. So I packed up and went to Los Angeles and bought and sort of produced my first feature film, *Tunnel Vision*, featuring many actors from the cast of *Saturday Night Live*'s first season.

Turned out, I was lucky on my maiden film voyage and *Tunnel Vision* was the biggest independent film in its day.

But the lessons never ended. I had a hit film, but how do I collect my money?

I remember being at my first film convention just after *Tunnel Vision*'s release and running into a drive-in movie theater owner who proudly shook my hand when we were introduced; "I want to thank you for *Tunnel Vision*, I bought a brand new Mercedes Benz on your share of the box office that you will never collect!"

DREAMS CAN COME TRUE BUT COLLECTIONS CAN BE A BITCH!

Here's the deal:
You must chase your own dreams *and*
They may change many times along the way.
They may even turn out to arrive even at a different place than you originally envisioned.
There is a certain skill set that starts to become obvious.
A certain sense that you are good or great at a particular aspect of your trade.

I don't think that it is just the actual business sector that matters.

IT IS THE SKILLS THAT YOU PERFECT ALONG THE WAY.

In my case, I realized as a promoter, a film and TV producer and director, that I was best at taking a vision and bringing it to fruition. My mistake along my train line was not leveraging success within the same sector. After six years of successfully producing and directing *Night Flight*, I had mastered the art of producing tons of original quality cable television and I was on top of my game.

So what I do? I quit, gave up my rights and move to Brazil and try to produce movies again.

It's true that my second big dream at that point of my life was to produce movies and not more cable television.

I was always a film producer, and influential in getting movies made, finished, and distributed, and felt that television was a compromised medium, even though I had become skilled and accomplished at my trade.

Restlessness wasn't fatal but it was not well thought out.

True, I came back and produced *Mondo New York*, which I feel is one of my major career accomplishments, however, I lost the leverage of having mastered the cable television universe. And I was a recognized pioneer at that time.

THE TRICK WITH CREATIVITY IS TO KEEP IT AT THE CENTER OF YOUR GRAVITATIONAL PULL BUT NOT LET IT DISTRACT YOU AWAY FROM THE COURSE OF YOUR MAINSTAY.

My creativity drove me to *Mondo*. New York. I needed total freedom and control, which I no longer had in cable television.

What I lost was the leverage of success and ease of stride in the workflow of my creativity.

Now, years later, I am so lucky to be back with *Night Flight*.

My *Night Flight* opportunity has an interesting twist of wisdom.

After six years of producing 16 hours of *Night Flight* every weekend, I decided that I needed to get out of New York City because I wanted to raise my newborn son Dorian in an environment that was free of the Rock and Roll drug scene. I made the fatal mistake of giving back my rights to my partner for a stupidly small amount of money.

For 30 years, I thought it was the single worst mistake of my career. As business life can sometimes bless you, I had the chance to buy back my rights a few years ago.

WHAT I LEARNED WAS:
NEVER GIVE UP YOUR RIGHTS! NEVER!

Creativity is not necessarily nurtured at a higher intensity just when something is new.

Creativity is such a momentary spark that it is not the application of the concept but the sparks and shocks that run the engine!

CREATIVITY HAS TO BE FED EVERY DAY.

CREATIVITY IS A WAY OF LIFE NOT A RANDOM EXPRESSION WE GET TO WHEN WE HAVE SOME EXTRA TIME.

MY EXPLORATIONS INTO
IMMORTALITY STEMMED MOSTLY
IN THE BEGINNING AROUND EARLY
LSD EXPERIENCES, during which
I could sense that the other side
of the life universe wasn't really
the other side, but more the
inside of my own universe.
Along the way, I started to glean
onto the sense that the road
inside immortality lay in space
between the atoms or
the silence between the notes.

THE GROWING AWARENESS THAT SO MUCH MORE OF THE ESSENCE OF LIFE,

and afterlife, was made up of this empty space, has given me a great sense that immortality and afterlife is full of that empty space. Just like it already exists inside us.

We just do not know how to understand empty space at the living moment of our lives.

After graduating and jumping into any chance to produce a concert and later a film or TV show, I started to realize if I raised my personal bar of accomplishments, I may be able to produce something that would "stand the test of time."

In those early days, the buzzword was "evergreen." The evergreen push was really a commercial and financial drive. I wanted to produce something that ran on TV for years, or a book or song that would be a hit and be selling for years over and over. But that aspiration has evolved into, what can I do to produce or create that moves the needle in society and still make a lightning bolt doing it.

It's not that immortality is actually a physical thing, but more an accomplishment that I can look at it in the context of worthiness.

I am not talking about great accomplishments, because I believe now when I walk down the street and give a homeless person money, I am touching immortality somehow.

It's pure acts of kindliness that can pierce the rainbow of immortality or at least an inner sense that a good act on the way to work creates a ripple in your universe that can beat on in its own way forever.

Having just spent time at a Buddhist retreat and receiving teachings from Robert Thurman and Gelek Rimpoche on various aspects of immortality, I have come to understand that immortality happens every day in everything we do, if we exercise the motivations of compassion for others and for ourselves.

This nexus of the creative quest to produce a great and evergreen product runs along the path of our spirit.

A copyright lasts 70 years after our death.

Great works of art, hundreds, maybe even thousands of years.

OUR SPIRIT AND SOUL WILL OUTLIVE ALL OUR MATERIAL EFFORTS.

I have been gauging my personal sense of immortality in such a material way that I neglected the true meaning of the quest and the goal.

Every day if we can produce ourselves in a pure and spiritually motivated fashion we ensure our immortality in a much higher sense.

Tolerance in the face of bullshit.
Taking the time and patience to help an associate when you feel inside they are being dumb and lazy.

BE BAMBOO IN THE WINDS OF FEAR AND ANGER

Creative rebirth in the ashes of failure.
Overcoming the will and weakness to quit a job before finishing.

ENJOY THE STRENGTH THAT GROWS FROM THE TREE OF BROKEN LIMBS.

AND BELIEVE WE ARE ALL IMMORTAL.

THE SUNDAY NEW YORK TIMES SAT ON MY COUCH FOR TWO WEEKS UNREAD, PERFECTLY TOGETHER.

Unable to sleep at 5AM this morning, I grabbed it with a sense of no value because it was old news and started to throw it out. Sensing maybe I should just check out my favorite sections of Travel and Art before trashing the old news, I found an article on Edward Curtis, the famous Native American photographer from the 1890s.

BACK IN MY DAZE IN THE '70S, CURTIS PHOTOS SURFACED AND BECAME A GREAT SENSATION AMONG THE HIP STONERS.

I collected a stack of 20 for about $1,500 and have enjoyed many on my walls ever since.

Curtis is an intriguing example of a great artist with a mission of immortality driven by an inexhaustible talent and obsession to capture a lost world that was in the process of disappearing forever.

For more than 30 years, he photographed the American Indian in the West, amassing a treasure of 40,000 photos, which he published in a 20-volume set. Only 222 sets were published, and in the end, Curtis was bankrupt and blind, and died alone in a Los Angeles apartment at age 84.

DO YOU THINK CURTIS IS BLIND AND BROKE IN HEAVEN?

Curtis left behind an immortal work that in a thousand years will be as precious as the King James Edition of the Bible and the masterpieces of Rembrandt and Beethoven.

Curtis was an artist with a singular vision and passion that guided his entire artistic life.

It's hard to equalize pain and suffering and personal material failure with monumental artistic achievement.

I am sure as soon as his body vessel started to pass into the other side of the spiritual world

He was welcomed with the applause and

Jubilation of a Great Master surrounded by

Adorning Throngs of Spirits

Thanking him for his Performance in Life.

The road to Artistic and Creative Fulfillment is Littered with Pain.

SUCCESS AND DISAPPOINTMENT SUCCESS AND POVERTY ARE THE MARRIAGE OF TALENTED FORCES

Anyone who has experienced making a movie can testify to that weird mixture at the end of exhaustion, exhilaration, and usually no money left.

REMEMBER IT'S NOT THE END GAME. IT'S THE GAME.

The end probably comes in the spirit world, which is free from the material restrictions of the scales with which we weigh our projects.

The wonderful component of the Daily Process is that
It really is close to the Spirit World in the Material World.

WE HAVE TO FINISH OUR PROJECTS.

We have to Print it.
We have to Publish it.
We have to Distribute it.
No matter how Painful or Financially Problematic.

Unfinished projects are tenants that are more destructive than the pain to get to the finish line.
Unfinished projects can be the seeds of cancer if they linger too long.

The only chance of immortal creativity is the final product, even with all its flaws and blemishes.

CURTIS LIVES FOREVER.
HE IS RICH AND NO LONGER BLIND

CHARITY DOES NOT BEGIN AT HOME.

CHARITY BEGINS IN OUR HEART.

In our formative years, most of us were indoctrinated by some formal attempt of religious templates to teach us how to be good spiritual citizens in relation to our fellow brothers and sisters. Somehow, most of us repudiate that strategy and get confused along the way between Religion, God, and Spirituality.

AND THEN, ON THE WAY TO WORSHIP, WE LOSE OUR GRIP OR GLIMMER OF WHAT GOD IS,

and further confuse ourselves between our Parent's Religion and their Culture and what is our own Religion and Culture.

I was pretty lucky during my test years to discover the spiritual world and other worlds during my acid trips. The discovery of a vivid plasma world unattached to any physical reality, allowed me to connect with a strong sense of human connectivity that generated a permanent sense of compassion for all lost street beings that I encounter.

I accepted early on that in my own small way I would Try to never pass a homeless person without giving some money. Sometimes it's a quarter or a dollar, and sometimes its my last $5 bill in my wallet
And Yes the Try overcomes the laziness inside.

I still can walk by and don't feel The Give.

But it does not make me feel good in that after second of inner dialogue.

When I give on my way to work, it really makes me feels good about my journey and myself for the day.

Street donations can get seriously complicated in some regions of the world, but for the most part in my urban wanderings I like to give. I also try to say, "God bless you" when I do give.

In the last decade, my wife Laurie, and I have tried to donate to our best friend's charity, A Glimmer of Hope.
Five Thousand dollars is about enough to build one new water well in Ethiopia.

I love the water well story because it has such a direct contribution impact that we can see and realize personally.

Without question, the reward for a direct charity donation that can be measured and visualized is an extraordinary emotional self-realization.

And it does touch an Act of Immortality.

Even though I consider myself somewhat generous, I don't think I really touch the capacity of what I should be doing or how much more impact I could generate if I focused more on it.

Giving money to charity is a kind act, one that we should all participate in to the best of our financial ability.

However, I believe the more important issue is how we incorporate our time and our Creative Talent to benefiting organizations that could use Our Skills—more than our money.

I often worry that if I were to prematurely die, that I would have seriously fucked up, because I would not have applied enough of my talent to help my fellow earthly citizens.

Sometimes an act of advocacy to make society a better place is equivalent, if not more valuable, than individual acts of charity.

Of course, this can be seriously convoluted when advocacy crosses the line into political action and persuasion. We have to be careful not to mix them up.

DON'T BULLSHIT YOUR SELF.

With social media and technology there is a new convergence of acts for social good and there are wonderful opportunities to make a difference, with Impact like never before in history.

IT IS IMPORTANT
TO BUILD AN EARLY
HABIT OF SPIRITUAL
COMPASSION
DEEP INSIDE AND
REALIZE THAT WE ARE
ALL CONNECTED—
MORE THAN EVER.

The Impact of Internet connectivity gives us a great and unique opportunity to have an Impact during the day with minimal distraction from our day jobs.

But a simple tweet is not necessarily an Act of engagement and that
In order to Make a Difference,
We need a Commitment and Immersive Engagement in the
Process and
The Outcome and
The Aftermath.

ALWAYS GIVE AND ACTIVATE WITHOUT ANY NEED FOR A RESPONSE OR THANKS.

Our Hearts have a Wonderful Mechanism to Reward our Inner Self in a Natural State.
It's Biblical to Give without Expectation other than the Act Itself.

DIGITAL RAPE ON MY DIGITAL SOUL.

It comes out of nowhere and is one of the new sensations of the 21st century Age of Lost Innocence.

I joined a special tier or as my friends boast, special enough to wear The Anonymous Badge of Honor.

I'VE BEEN HACKED

Son of a
Junk Man,
Rocketeer
G Man for the J Men Forever

In my Daze,
Anonymous would have been pot dealers trying to get
everyone turned on.

I got hacked
NOT for being bad,
Not for being illegal,
Not for crossing the line,
Just for being
Sloppy,
Stupid,
Sleepy and
Not paying attention to details.

HACKERS ARE LIKE WATER

Water can seep in if the foundation is not Water Proof
Structurally sound and
Up to Date.

But the damage can always be mitigated by
Constant Preparation and
Attention to Detail.

There is a saying in the film business:
How do movies get made?
Preparation.
Preparation.
Preparation.
Over the years I have repeatedly used this phrase in every
context possible to express the need for Exercise in the Art
of Life and Business.

There's not much difference between getting hacked and
Getting hit by a car because you traveled too late through a
Changing Yellow Traffic Light.
Both could have been avoided
With Better Concentration.

The difference between 2017 and 1964 is that everything travels
faster, and that really means that your attention to detail and
focus on the small shit has to be so much tighter, stronger, vigilant!

We are all Fighting in a
Digital War Without Bullets.

Transparency can easily create a Digital Immortality
and this is a good thing.

In my day, we had pay phones!
No NSA recording of our conversations
It was easy to be anonymous.
Paper Ruled.

LIFE IN THE WORLD OF DIGITAL WARFARE FORCES US **TO THINK BEFORE WE POST.** IT WILL LAST FOREVER.

Living in the mouth of a Digital Lion that can cause long-term harm or embarrassment must force us to consider our digital actions in new ways of self-preservation and protection. And many actions don't come to roost until many years later.

The seeds of embarrassment can take a long time to grow… so beware of what you plant.

Here's the positive side:
In the age of transparency and no limits on privacy,
The awareness of ourselves
Our inner persons
Our core self-system
Will be so clearly exposed that we will have less defenses to grow from who we really are.

In many ways, most of us struggle all our lives to get away or hide who we are, or who we want to be, but in the 21st century, that wall of defensive protection is openly and constantly broken into.

This is good because it rids us of our own bullshit to hide within ourselves and therefore get on with it, support it, and grow the core of Who we really are.

REMEMBER:
HAPPINESS AND SUCCESS CAN ONLY
COME FROM
- ► EXPLOITING
- ► BUILDING
- ► GROWING AND
- ► MANIFESTING OUR CORE SELVES AND OUR CORE CREATIVE FOUNDATION.

CREATIVE COURAGE OVERCOMES ALL OBSTACLES!

I REMEMBER WHEN I WAS REALLY YOUNG AND BORROWED MONEY FROM SOMEONE AND COULD NOT PAY IT BACK, I would avoid a face-to-face encounter and run the other way.
There was no way to avoid going through life without credit and almost just as hard to avoid loans from friends and family.

What I learned long ago is that some small payment toward a debt is the way to keep a negative on the positive side.

Small token payments are much better than none at all.

Often we hold off because we don't have the correct total owed, so we neglect and postpone, and more times than not, that amount never gets held onto and gets used for expenses other than the debt.

Also, token payments add up over time and make the final overdue amount easier to attain.

We all have a tendency to run to the avoidance side rather than the proactive, in-your-face side. I can only say that after all these years, the harder the shit falls the more valuable it is to fear not your friends and supporters.

TRANSPARENCY AND TOTAL HONESTY IS WHAT GENERATES THE GREATEST LEVERAGE.

I think that your personality wraps around transparency as a committed platform and frees us from defensive excuses and making up stories to cover our Asses.

The facts are usually pretty much the same: we can't pay, for whatever reason.

IF WE CAN'T PAY, IT'S BETTER TO BE RELIABLE THROUGH TRUTH, AS IT IS THE ONLY WAY TO BUILD TRUST WHEN SHIT HITS THE FAN.

AND SHIT **ALWAYS** HITS THE FAN.

REJECTION NEVER CEASES TO INFLICT ITS PAIN. WHAT AMAZES ME IS HOW IT CAN ATTACH ITSELF TO SUCCESS. It comes in all colors. The obvious component is when rejection is surrounded by failure in business or creative endeavors. When we fail, it is easier to digest rejection as part of the process, though not any easier to dispel.

THE ONE THAT STILL PERPLEXES ME IS WHEN I AM BESET BY **REJECTION THE SAME TIME I AM ENJOYING A SUCCESS.**

Rejection is a Natural Part of the Process.

The Nighttime and Daytime of a career.

The trick to the release from the Rejection Platform is to
Turn it into positive energy, and
To beat back the negative component of its darkness.

I can still remember negative reviews of some of my
commercially successful film releases and the hardship of
understanding that my personal taste in films was really
disturbing to many in the mainstream. But having made a
career of producing and distributing edgy, cult entertainment,
I knew that most of my experiences were going to be rejections.

My first film, *Tunnel Vision*, "Wasn't a movie, just a collection
of short vignettes made from video."

For *Tarzoon, Shame of the Jungle,* "It should be thrown into a snake pit along with the negative."

When one of the performers in *Mondo New York* bit the head of a rat as a performance piece, I received rat parts in the mail for a year.

The negative reviews never really stopped. They were just a natural part of life, living and producing in the Cutting Edge.

I learned very early on that if I was going to cut the edge of life,

The only success was going to be the process of doing it.

There was always going to be something that was disappointing and cruel at the end of the cycle.

REJECTION NEVER STOPS

You think you have just produced a great PowerPoint and you have a misspelling that nobody saw along the way.
Not exactly rejection but still that inner sense that you fucked up and could have or should have seen it, even though you stared at it for a week.

Recently I noticed the word "management" was misspelled as "managment" on a sales one-sheet that had 1,000 prints and was out for six months!

And nobody noticed it.
Not rejection but still
A Strange Sense of Failure.

The lesson is to step away from everything and come back and look slowly at every word, every aspect.

ASSUME IN THE BEGINNING THAT YOU WILL MAKE A MISTAKE

Assume in the beginning you will be rejected.
Assume you will misspell something.
Assume the contract you just finished will have something left out that you will feel really stupid about in six months.

ASSUMPTION IS THE MOTHER OF FUCK UP. ASSUME YOU WILL FUCK UP.

It will prevent some of the Fuck Ups along the way.

But assuming you are going to Fuck Up in the beginning is a good thing for the process.

TO BUILD ENERGY FROM REJECTION IS A LIFELONG PURSUIT. REJECTION IS THE SEED OF YOUR NEXT CREATIVE SURGE

Never stop to fight back against the outside world that will always think you are not special and precious.
Not perfect enough.
Not on the inside team.
Maybe, like me, you are in the service and software business, and you have to deal every day with customers who think you don't do enough for them.

Plant a stake in the heart of that rejection code.
Take that energy and
Move it on to Recreate.

Assume it's all just a part of the Positive Process.
Rejection is like taking a good shit in the morning.

EMPTY YOURSELF.

MAKE WAY AND ROOM FOR A NEW MEAL.

MOST OF US USE A SCALE
ON A REGULAR BASIS TO WATCH
OUR WEIGHT AND REGULATE OUR INTAKE,
OR AT LEAST TRY TO.
We are conditioned to weighing
ourselves as a physical gauge.

We have money
Salaries
Interest rates
Taxes at all kinds of levels.
Capital Gains
Capital Losses

On a daily basis, we gauge, calculate, and use all kinds of metrics to evaluate our status.

WHAT IS THE SCALE TO WEIGH OUR HAPPINESS?

What do we use to evaluate our success besides how much money we are earning?

I have come to believe that the Impact Scale is one of the most important scales that I need to evaluate, weigh, and reflect my energy flow.

It's not a scale I can jump on and weigh some number.
It's a recognition scale
A consciousness scale
A meditative scale to have inner thoughts
Inner dialogue
A partner dialogue

The Impact Scale is a way to infuse my daily exercise of life with a new inner dialogue.

Instead of "Hi Sweetheart, how was your day?"

It's "Hi My Love, how was your Impact today?"

I am starting to look at my Impact on a daily basis.

Starting to focus,

Be more conscious

More Aware of the effects of

My Actions,

My Creativity, and

My Goals.

IMPACT CAN TAKE ON MANY VARIATIONS.

I recently bought a painting from an English painter, William Bradley. When my wife and I hung his painting in our living room, we had the distinct feeling that it enriched our lives. I wrote to William and told him how his single work of art could enrich and be so impactful. He wrote back confirming that such gratitude and impact was the most important result he could achieve from his art and creativity.

William, the artist, creates great works of art that enjoy only a small universe of impact, sometimes one to one or one to few. Nonetheless, William's art, and therefore William, produces great Impact.

An example of charitable Impact, both personal and communal, is a donation to Charity: Water or A Glimmer of Hope help to build a single water well in a region in Ethiopia that has never had free running water…this act of Impact will change the lives of 500 individuals for generations.

A social media campaign by a 15-year-old girl successfully convinced Pepsico and Coca-Cola to remove brominated vegetable oil from their Powerade and Gatorade products and created an Impact that benefited millions of people for maybe generations.

My wife Laurie worked for two years on a book, *Dr. Mao's Secrets of Self-Healing*. She was disappointed by what seemed to be its limited success. In many ways, books can be long and hard roads to produce, and most of the time, only small numbers of readers are reached.

How do we gauge low Impact and the success factor?
How do we justify years later the reason we pursued that project?

In Laurie's case, several years after her book was released, we were at a Dr. Mao event, and a woman spoke to the group, recounting how she found out she had cancer, lost her job, lost her insurance, but found *Dr. Mao's Secret's of Self-Healing* and studied it and intensely followed its recommendations.
One year later, her cancer was in remission.

I turned to Laurie and asked, "Was it worth it to save one life?"
She confirmed with a high five.

Impact can be Local,

Contained,

Wide, and Global.

THE MOST IMPORTANT INGREDIENT IS TO **BECOME AWARE OF WHAT YOU DESIRE YOUR IMPACT TO BE.**

WHAT ARE YOUR IMPACT REASONS?
**CAN YOU ADJUST YOUR STRATEGY
TO CREATE GREATER IMPACT?**

REFOCUS SO THAT IMPACT
HAS GREATER EFFICIENCY.

BE CONSCIOUS OF YOUR IMPACT.
IT'S A SCALE TO CARRY YOUR WHOLE LIFE.

LAST NIGHT, WE TRAVELED OUT
AS A PARTY OF FOUR.
Two couples, One car, and it wasn't
my car. I found myself at the end of the
night and on the third-party location,
way past midnight and had enough.
And like a very unhappy and hungry
child, I lost my cool because
I was stuck on my own path and
there was no Uber that could save me.

CONTROL YOUR RIDE IS A METAPHOR FOR CONTROLLING YOUR SPACE.

Be aware of the circumstances and don't let the flow of others put you in a compromising position you are stuck with.

We get stuck all the time,
We get stuck with partners,
Stuck with lovers,
Stuck with asshole bosses,
Stuck with drunk drivers.
I always remember hounding my kid to not be a rider in
a drunken car and instead to walk away.
Have NO fear of walking away.
Control your ride in life and never fear the peer pressure to go
along when in your heart you know it's a mistake.

THERE IS ALWAYS SOMETHING BETTER ON THE OTHER SIDE OF NO.

My wife and I were taking a taxi the other day on Park Avenue and stopped at a red light and Brian, Laurie's youngest son, just walked in front of us.

RANDOM QUANTUM ATTRACTION.

I felt like I was in the Pulp Fiction scene when Jules walks in front of Butch just when he is getting away.

I have been commuting between New York and D.C. and New York and L.A. for years, and I am always amazed to find that if I make the effort to engage the person sitting next to me, most of the time it's someone of interest.

What amazes me most is the frequency of meeting people I know by randomly bumping into them.

What does that really mean?

When I have that experience, it reinforces my belief in universal connectivity, which naturally makes me feel universally spiritual and in a funny way, immortal.

I HAVE ALWAYS USED THE EXPRESSION: HAVE TO BE IN THE BALLPARK, PLAYING THE GAME, AND AT BAT, FOR SOMETHING TO HAPPEN.

It's hard sometimes to strike up a conversation, but I have found it always worthwhile to probe and be progressively social.

When we are travelling in the same track side by side, I assume there is something similar and almost always interesting about that person next to me.

For much of my recent life, I have grown to be a hybrid technology evangelist and an innovative salesman. As such, I lost all inhibition to meet and introduce myself to various members of Congress on shuttles between New York City and D.C. Many times, I have admittedly changed my seat so that I could sit next to someone of importance.

One time, on the shuttle from D.C., I was boarding and talking to another passenger when I noticed that a VIM (Very Important Member) had an empty seat next to her and it was not mine. Without hesitation, I quickly asked the other passenger if I could switch with him, and voila I enjoyed a unique opportunity that came from a shared plane ride.

Which brings me to another, important goal:
Strive to Fly First or Business Class and
Never give up the First Class Quest.
Life is series of Coach, Business, and First Class Events.

First Class is an inside lifestyle, not just a seat on a plane.
It's clean water through a filter in your kitchen or your shower.
It's Organic instead of Choice.

We work our asses off for lots of reasons, but in my world the main reason to make dough is to be able to live in first class.

First or business class is
Good for your body,
Your self-esteem and
Good for business.

There is no doubt that most of time, the person next to me
is worth having a conversation with.
And many times, it can really be a business-landing opportunity.

FIRST CLASS IS NOT JUST AN UPGRADE, FIRST CLASS IS A WAY OF LIFE.

First class can be in a tent.
There are first class tents now at festivals.

It can be the quality of a pillow.
One thousand-count sheets.

A striving for everything we do and
All things in the physical matrix.

We should always want to hear
He or She is a First-Class Individual.

I RECENTLY VISITED RICK NIELSEN,
THE LEADER OF CHEAP TRICK,
WHO HAS TO BE ONE OF THE GREAT ROCK
AND ROLL COLLECTORS OF ALL TIME.
Rick started collecting every poster,
boarding pass, and bits of writing
since he started his rock and roll career.

More importantly, Rick started collecting guitars in the beginning of his career and has mostly kept every one he ever purchased. Today, Rick has a treasure trove of guitars that may well be one of the greatest collections in the world.

The value of collecting and keeping your items safe and organized has many rewards. The Emotional Dividends are Everlasting.

Looking back on my life, I can break down collecting wisdom into several aspects:

First, keep your baseball cards!

Not many of us have the luxury to have a parents' attic to store our shit untouched for decades.

Either way, start with a strong, waterproof and airtight box to protect your collectables as you move in your early years.

Get a portfolio case to hold papers and posters to ensure your posters stay flat. I noticed that Rick actually placed a lot of his posters on a cardboard backing in a sealed collapsible folder. Very smart.

THE MOST IMPORTANT ASPECT THOUGH IS TO **COLLECT WHAT YOU LOVE AND WHAT GIVES YOU PLEASURE.**

And don't let your spouse, your girlfriend, your parent throw out your shit.

I have kept a garage with my son, Dorian, as co-conspirator, at his Mom's house for 25 years. When his Mom was selling her house and had to empty the garage, I confronted Dorian who was willing to throw out much more than I was.
Many items he no longer thought were worthy of holding, and did not want to have to throw them out as meaningless in 20 more years.

Time will tell if they have meaning. When I am long gone his kids can have a better idea where we all came from and what we were all about.

The second most important thing is to buy quality and not be afraid of overpaying for great stuff.

It's hard thinking in today's dollar amounts and to think that in 20, 30, 40 years, you could be well rewarded.

Rick told me when he bought a certain guitar for $7,000 40 years ago, it was an enormous amount of money to pay for an old guitar. Today that guitar is worth hundreds of thousands.

Quality Always Pays Off In the End!

I could have bought an Andy Warhol in 1970 for not much more than Rick paid for his guitar and we all know how many millions that could have paid off.

I just read that if you bought $1,000 in Wal-Mart stock when it went public and kept it, it would be worth millions today.

The rule is simple.
Start collecting when you're young.
Keep everything and
Keep it in good condition and
Keep it Flat!

Always buy the best pieces and always pay more rather than less.

Never walk away from a deal because the seller did not come down to your price.

Time will always make the money spent on an overpaid item seem trivial.

BELIEVE IN YOUR TASTE AND BELIEVE IN YOUR VISION.

If you buy and sell stock, set aside some shares and never sell them.

I FIRST MET ALAN DOUGLAS,
OR AD AS WE CALLED HIM, OUTSIDE
THE BOTTOM LINE IN THE VILLAGE,
after a performance by Betty Davis
(Miles Davis' wife aka Black Betty).
He was with his wife and soon to be
my wife, Stella, and I was with my
best friend Michael Lang.

I WAS A KID OF 26 AND HE WAS A LEGEND OF 42.

At the time, I thought AD was a million years older than me.
I was the Kid and AD was the Master.

How is it in life that a man or woman can be your brother out of
blood and yet so much more than a blood brother can give you?

I think anyone who can become an inside treasure of our heart,
profoundly related in spirit, and bound by unconditional love,
must be a spirit that we have already been related
to in other lifetimes.

Next comes the attention and commitment to flourish the bond.

The rewards of a great brotherhood with our few selected heart
brothers and sisters are most likely to be the most rewarding
treasures of love and friendship.

If we are lucky,
Once in a lifetime,
To love, and
Come to be loved by a Master,
Then Fear Not,

Waste Not.
Life is Short and
Masters tend to be busy individuals.

Jimi Hendrix was the one who gave Alan his nickname AD.
Jimi always joked it stood for After Death.
So if you love enough, and pursue the commitment to great
friendship then you might have your own AD.

AD was special because he was uncompromising in the state
of production and physical boundaries.

After getting married to Stella Douglas, AD's wife of many
years, he took me under his wing, and taught me
Line by Line,
Mix by Mix,
Edit by Edit,
Color by Color,
Font by Font and
With an unbridled quest for perfection in his product,
he fashioned his kid brother into a matrix of a
Passion for Creativity and
Young consciousness of the quantum effect of
The never-ending pursuit of an
Uncompromised Finished Product.
AD's Last Marching Orders Were:

NEVER COMPROMISE
IN THE CREATIVE JOURNEY.

When I was producing *Night Flight*, and seriously indulged into
maximum output of production, AD used to come by the studio
regularly to visit. I had mastered a unique formula for producing
and broadcasting more than 20 hours a week of television.
And in those daze we were only analogue.

AD would show me the other side of life, and
Spend days mixing and editing a single track.

I look back now and better understand that great product
The kind of product that touches Creative Immortality,
Only comes when there is a combination of
Genius talent and
Impeccable Uncompromising Attention
to the Production Detail.

Yes, Freshness of a Talent:
Records or a book or a live event that has special timing can
make it more likely a product can be great!

THERE ALWAYS HAS TO BE
A GREAT PRODUCER
BEHIND EVERYTHING.

Alan Douglas was a genius producer in all aspects.
What the fuck is a producer anyway?

Recognizing talent.
Attracting talent.
Inspiring talent.

You seize an opportunity that is embedded with real talent and
Forge a relationship of Trust and Support that becomes
mutually creative; greater than the individual talent can
manifest alone.
Demanding the Rewards of Creative Collaboration.

AD knew talent instantly, whether it was a Jazz Genius like
Duke, Dolphy, or Coleman, or Rock, like Jimi.

The second most important quality is to
STAY YOUNG!
FEAR NO CHANGES

Pursue your Unbridled Passion for the New and the Next.

AD was always young in his creative pursuit.
Creatively critical until his last words of wisdom.

My whole life, I have been perplexed by the concept of creating immortality in a product. I have come to recognize that it can only come from the rare occasions of genuinely collaborative genius talent being at the same place and time, driven by a producer who can speculate creative alchemy with a vision and courage to make it happen, always in the face of uncertain odds.

The great composers and writers are true examples
of immortality.
Surely, when it comes to music there are many examples of immortal greatness.

AD achieved immortality with numerous records.
What a lucky man I was to be mentored and loved and shared so much with a man who created immorality.

YEARS AFTER BEING HACKED
THE REPERCUSSIONS ARE STILL
BEING FELT.
Like the after effects of a strong
earthquake, the aftershock on the
ecosystem is still obvious.

I AM LEARNING THAT BRUISES MAY LOOK LIKE THEY HAVE HEALED ON THE OUTSIDE,

but that we possess a strong tendency to de-focus on the root causes of the symptom that showed itself.

Just fixing the immediate system breach, whether it is a bruise, a tumor, or a break is only temporary relief from the obvious. The trick is to stay focused on what appears to be healthy, and assume that no matter what you see, or what you feel, or don't feel, inside it there is always something dysfunctional.

How do we transform defensive energy spent on fixing and reacting into positive energy spent on proactive awareness and transparent self-action?

Do we go through that yellow to red light because we are lazy? Because we are defiant?
Or are we stupid because we are tempting odds that immediately shift against us?

Systematic issues, even if they are easily fixed, are one of the best examples of knowing that the ecosystem is not properly functioning.

So what happens when shit is happening and just doesn't stop?

WE ARE ALL ADDICTS OF PROCRASTINATION AND DENIAL.

How do we trigger a new awareness and acceptance so that change can make things better?

It has become more and more clearer that

THE ONLY ROAD TO SUCCESS AND TO FREEDOM STARTS WITH SELF-AWARENESS AND ACCEPTANCE.

Once we come clean to ourselves, we can express it openly, without freaking out.

Then everything starts to fall into place.

We are creatures of Fear of Change.

How many times have I heard:

"I don't know what he does, so I am afraid to get rid of him?"

In film production, when there is a very short and expensive schedule, if someone is not working out, no time is wasted on replacement. Fired and replaced without hesitation! Yet in business, we tend to take too long to execute.

When it comes to Ourselves on Ourselves,
We are the worst to fix ourselves when we are fucking up
Even though inside we know it.

My brother-in-law always told me, with a sense of glee
and freedom,

"I HAVE NEVER MISSED SOMEONE I FIRED AFTER THREE MONTHS."

THE JEWISH NEW YEAR, ROSH HASHANAH, **IS CELEBRATED FOR** TWO DAYS. The first is always considered the major day and the second day an extra repeat. Usually, most synagogues do not require a ticket to participate in the services on the second day.

THIS YEAR, LIKE MANY OTHERS PAST, I DECIDED TO GO ONLY ON THE SECOND DAY.

Walking from my apartment I could see Jews on their way to pray with kids in hand.

I arrive at my first choice, a very upscale East Side synagogue to be told, "No tickey no washy."
In my normal extra effort, I attempt to ask if I can speak to someone in the office. Total Rejection. Can't even buy a ticket!
The office manager suggests, "Try this free service," and hands me a flyer. Upon arrival at number two, I find it is only a service for the first day. Moving on and toward Fifth Avenue, I know I have several more choices.

Feeling a bit perplexed
A lost Jew in Manhattan
Trying to get my Jew fix
Feeling like an Oxymoron.

Walking down Fifth Avenue, I see an elderly man in short coat, no tie, but carrying a colorful blue yarmulke in his hand as he walks past me. I turn around and ask, "Excuse me, but do you know a synagogue around here that may accept no ticket to enter today?"

He says, "I have an extra ticket and please join me. I always get an extra ticket in case my son one day will join me."

And I am off, bathed in Jewish connectivity and gratitude for the situation.

It turns out to be a wonderful Orthodox service in the Metropolitan Museum, in the auditorium inside the Egyptian section. Quite an historical entrance to celebrate the birth of earth or is it mankind?

Here's the wisdom in the Journey
We are Going to Get Rejected All the Time.
We Reject Ourselves Even Before We Act.
That inner Awareness of Our Mind
Interacting with Itself and
Realizing that we are Not Acting on Pure Instinct.

It's at the very moment that
The Inner Rejection Journey Starts that
We have to become Acutely More Aware of the
Signs and Details that Pass in Front of Us.
And we have to be willing to stop in our momentum and
reverse course.

TO ASK
TO CONFRONT
TO BE CURIOUS
TO EXPRESS
TO FIND ANOTHER PATHWAY

Had I not looked closely
To see the Yarmulke in the hand walking by and
To Be Willing to Turn Around and
To Not be
Too shy
To interrupt a stranger

I May Never Have Had a Genuine Mystical and Spiritually
Rewarding Experience.

And the best of all was a confirmation that we do have direct
influence over our fate, and the simplest of actions can affect
a new outcome of events.

I JUST LIVED THROUGH
A YELLOW LIGHT EXPERIENCE.
Driving home from the airport,
not speeding, and really not in a hurry,
I pulled over on the side of the road
to make a U-turn to check out a barn
sale on the other side of the road.
There was a lot of traffic in the
opposite direction and I saw an opening
that was possible, but I needed
to accelerate more than normal to
get in ahead.

A CAR ACCIDENT

Only problem was, I did not look behind my left shoulder after
I checked my rearview mirror. I was making a too-quick decision
rather than a fully-conscious driving decision. I looked carefully
in my side view but I had already inched out and my mirror did
not properly show the road.

I jump on it for the turn and smash—luckily I catch only the tail
end of an A5, who expertly swerved aside to avoid hitting me
square on my driver's side which would have been
one painfully fatal blow!

My thought process failed me. I failed myself.

I made a mistake in the nanosecond of my mind rather than
being cautious and waiting for a guaranteed secure moment.

I was lucky, blessed to be stupid and get away with one.

I have written so often about that yellow light awareness and
that your brain actually tells you that you have gone too far into
the danger field, and yet

WHY CAN'T WE HOLD BACK
WHEN WE KNOW BETTER?
IS OUR BRAIN JUST LIKE OUR DICKS?

Why do they let us do stupid shit even though
We record the Mistake while it is Happening?

IT'S A BITCH.
I'M 69 AND IT'S STILL HAPPENING.

A FEW YEARS AGO MY SON DORIAN
WAS WAITING UNTIL THE END OF THE
DAY TO CALL ME AND WISH ME A
HAPPY FATHER'S DAY.

He lives on the West Coast and
I am on the East Coast, and he was
unconscious of the pain and anxiety
of waiting for your kid to tell you he
loves you.

WHEN HE FINALLY CALLED, HE JOKED THAT HE HAD UNTIL MIDNIGHT TO STILL BE WITHIN THE TIME ZONE OF CORRECTNESS.

I almost didn't take his call.
But of course, love and fatherly compassion won over my anger.
I decided to write him a Father's Day Ethics Love Letter.

I explained in detail that early recognition is the only way
to go in life.
It's not just the issue of getting it out of the way.
The Early Thank You.
The Early I Love You Dad.
The Early I Love You Mom
The Quick Thank You for the dinner treat or meeting.

Even a handwritten note mailed the old fashion way goes so
much further.
He used to say: "I wanted to write a nice
Thank You but weeks passed and I forgot."

I say
Send a Quick Text,
A Quick Email and
Then write something longer.

TWO RULES:

► NEVER LET 24 HOURS GO BY WITHOUT A THANK YOU, NO MATTER HOW SHORT.

► SEND BIRTHDAY AND HOLIDAY GREETINGS FIRST THING IN THE DAY.

It's really hard to imagine how we as parents wait with anxiety to hear from our love buds.

I can still remember coming home at 4AM and my Mom would be sitting on the couch waiting for me and all
she would say was,

"ONE DAY YOU WILL UNDERSTAND."

WE ALL MARRY IN LOVE
LOVE TILL DEATH DO US PART
The very thought that our marriage
will not last is the farthest from our
minds when we first marry.
Our children are mostly conceived in
Love within the confines of marriage
That magical GOD given moment that
brings the Spark of Life

TO PROCREATE IS THE ESSENCE OF LIFE AND LOVE.

How is it that along the way
Marriage,
Love, and the
Pursuit of the Perfect Union finds itself
Out of Harmony?

How do two people once totally in Love fall apart into Madness?

Many events can trigger that downward spiral.

Sometimes a single event can be so destructive that you jump over the the line and give up hope and mutual support of the family union never wanting to go back.

We all make mistakes.

We get horny and cheat because our dicks lead us astray.

We drink too much and lose sight of the consequences.

We get fucked up on drugs and don't realize who we become in those moments of madness.

We let fantasies over take realty.

We lie to cover up, when transparency would be better served.

The primary issue is whether our mistakes are systemic and a factor of chronic behavior or just honest onetime fuck ups.

I will Love You
For Better or
For Worse
Does Worse mean stay with your husband if he beats you or your children?

Does Worse mean stay with your wife if she cheated on you with your best friend.

Does Worse mean throw out your husband because he cheated on you with your best friend?

Once?
Many Times?
Can't Stop?

There is Holy Responsibility that we all Pledge in our
Vows of Marriage to each other.
That responsibility to one another has nothing to do with the
responsibility and vows we take on with our children
once we have them.

"WHAT THE FUCK
WERE YOU THINKING?"
"DID YOU EVER THINK OF ME?"

"You Selfish Prick!"
Asks the Child of a Divorced Parent.

What are our responsibilities when we find ourselves in a
marriage burdened with fighting and
Stressed with Unhappiness?

Do Our Children Come First?
Or
Do We Come First?

Experience seems to dictate that divorce with children is a
selfish act that
BOTH parents indulge in.
My parent's generation did not believe in divorce. Many of them
stayed in unhappy marriages their whole lives.

And always because of the children.

It's a mysterious dilemma.

I am a divorced man from a woman I never stopped loving.
Who never stopped loving me.
With a child that was clearly harmed by his parents' irrational
behavior on many fronts.

Yet I found a second wife that enriched the second tier of my
life and love in ways
I could never have imagined.

Did I act selfishly and without regard
to what we were doing to our son?
Did we realize how self obsessed our personal behavior
was and how destructive it was to Love and Marriage
And the commitment to maintain a Perfect Union?
Absolutely NOT!

Were we Selfish and Blind?
Absolutely!

Why do we reach so easily for the exit trigger without regard
to our children and what the outcome may produce?
Why don't Our Children come First and
Husband and Wife Second?

How does the Perfect Love Fuck Up?

How do we Blind ourselves so easily?

Marriage is Sacred.

Children are the Meaning of Life.

Why are our vows so easily dismissed in today's culture?

The Answer My Friend Lies in

THE DAILY PURSUIT OF HONESTY AND THE PURSUIT OF CONSCIOUS AWARENESS OF WHO WE ARE AND WHAT WE DO EVERY DAY

How we talk to our Wife or Husband

How we Treat our Children with Love and Tenderness.

How we tell all our Love Ones

I LOVE YOU.

How we admit that we Fucked Up
Instead of Hiding the Truths

Until they become Self Evident
Much Too Late.
It is not an issue of if we go astray
But what we do to Rebound from Transgression.

How we become aware of our greedy and petty drives for
Superficial Gratifications.

Warning:
Don't throw in the towel even if there is an alternative
that is attracting you.

GO THE EXTRA MILE FOR YOUR KIDS. YOUR RESPONSIBILITY IS GREATER THAN THAT BLOW JOB.

Work at it.
Once in Love.
Always in Love.
Commitments of Love are Religious.
Commitments to Our Children are Sacred.
Remember you are the Mother and Father
of Your Children for Life
Born From Love
In Need of Love

IF **DIVORCE**
DIVORCE IN **LOVE AND RESPECT**
TAKE THE HIGH ROAD

The Long Term Health of our Children are
More Important than
The Money
Or the Revenge.
Life is Long
Your Seeds Are Your Immortality
The Love that Creates Life
Lives Forever

Protect the Bond that Created Love
Even if YOU can't live with that person anymore.

MAMA
PAPA
CHILDREN
ARE FOREVER

FRIENDSHIP IS KIN TO LOVE
AT FIRST SIGHT.
We can trace those
Glimmers of Love Lights
that capture the
First look of Love.
Lifelong Friends also have that
Magic Moment of Recognition.

FRIENDSHIP REWARDS

Aged in time
Become more
Rich and Precious.
Only if they are
Pro-Actively Engaged by
Both of Us.

As I write this, I find myself in
Dublin, attending the funeral of
My Best Friend's Dad.

Always wanted to visit Ireland
But never got it together
Until I dropped everything and
Jumped on a flight the next day.

Luckily the Funeral was postponed a couple of days and
I had the good opportunity
To be a Real Good Friend.

I used to think that
Just Showing Up Was Enough.
The Act of the Effort was the
The Main Ingredient.

On this Trip learned something New.
Of course I learned that Guinness Beer is the
Best Beer in the World.
For sure according to the Irish.

Seriously though,
I learned that Just Showing Up is
Not Good Enough
For
Real Good Friendship.

I learned that it takes
More Time in Learning about your Friend.

I learned that Friendship is
Taking the Extra Time
To go to your Friend's Hometown
No Matter Where in the World.

I learned that
Just Visiting,
Showing Up, and
Paying Your Respects are
Not Enough.
I learned that
Giving is also
Letting your friend
Give to You.

Creating the opportunity
To Allow your Friend
To Be able Share without Restriction.
Without a Time Limit.

Sometimes that takes More Time
Than we are Willing to Allocate
In our Busy Lives.

I learned that in
Heightened Emotions of
Loss
That Pain is Soothed when we can
Share about Ourselves to our
Best Friends.

I learned that when we share about
Our Childhood
Our Family
Our Mom and Dad
It Makes us Whole
It Heals
Even at moments of
Great loss.

All Life Experiences

Emotions

Love

And Life

Rest in our Head as

Memories

Past

Present

And Future

ENHANCING OURSELVES
OUR LOVED ONES
TAKES THE EXTRA EFFORT.

I learned that it is really

All about the

Extra Effort.

That's what makes

The Difference

In Friendship

In Life

In Love

In Health

In Success.

I learned that
Life is Fleeting.
And that
Friendship is Life.
And that it Lives
Outside Our Heads.

I LEARNED THAT THE REWARDS OF FRIENDSHIP ARE THE GIFT THAT NEVER STOP GIVING

And I learned that

I Love the Irish.

And Their Beer!

WHAT'S THE DIFFERENCE?
ARE YOU MISSING ANYTHING?
Chances are anyone reading
this will have gotten high already.
More than once.
Hopefully while you are reading this.

I HAVE GONE THROUGH EVERY STAGE OF DRUG GROWING UP.

I have been in jail on Acid in a foreign country and smoked Pot on a commerical airlines in the 70's with other passengers.
Back in those Daze, everyone smoked cigarettes on the plane.
Hard to imagine you could actually smoke in the bathroom and nobody gave a shit!

To clarify the dialogue of whatever wisdom I can glean from 50 years of blazing,
I think it's best to break this down into some basic drugs:
Pot
Coke
Pills
Tobacco
Alcohol-
Heroin-Opiates

Let's start with COKE.

Growing up as a young adult in the music biz in the '70s

Everyone was stoned on coke

All day

All night.

It was a culture that in a strange way was all tied together.

Coke is an intensely social drug with a

Strong sexual component.

We all carried coke on us like pocket change.

If you were a good or bad cokehead

You would most likely start the day off with a hit

Just like today you stop at Starbucks for your

Coffee Shot.

The great thing about coke was that it opened your creative

pathway in

An excessive fashion and allowed your sense and

Inside your brain to explore

Extreme journeys of possibility

Fueled by an intoxicated state of courage.

We did shit on coke

We dreamed of the sublime and ridiculous high on coke

Bold

Outrageous

Most of the time

Too far over the top.

I worked late nights for years in the video studios pumping out hundreds of hours of Night Flight.

Some of the most creative times in my life.
Not sure what they would have been like if we were all straight.
We were fucking crazy.

In those days, there was no digital postproduction. One-inch machines just arrived in 1981 and you could build a show using three playback one-inch machines and one recorder. The reels were all one hour long and Night Flight was a four-hour show that repeated itself for another four hours every Friday and Saturday night.
We had to build two four-hour shows, in real time, every week.
If we made a mistake, we had to re-record that section all over again.
It was brutal.
Studio 7PM–2AM four nights a week.
Plus daytime work in the office started for me at 11.
We smoked Pot
We snorted coke
We worked our Asses Off
We had a Fucking Blast
We brought a New World of Music and Culture to a
New Psychographic Generation.

THE DOWNSIDE OF **COKE** WAS THE DOWNSIDE.

The continuous Quest of the Coke High:

Even when you are already high

As High as you would ever want to get

And yet you Want More and More

THE DOWNSIDE IS THE HIGH.

There was never a way to just get high one time.

The insidious nature of this particular platform is

The drug controls you.

You don't control it!!

It makes you Lie to Your Self.

It's extraordinarily precocious.

The high is really there.

It opens up the world of possibilities.

But it's a False Spring Board.

There is something inside all of us that makes us attracted

to a drug like Coke.

It's the dark side for sure and yet it is terribly seductive.

The high always seemed momentary

Illusory

And then the other side of the mountain was

So painful and emotionally vapid.

It really does harm the straight part of us.

It's hard to accept a lot of the time that our ideas
and our actions when we were high
And Really High
Are Not Very Smart
So if we Indulge
We Must

KEEP AN HONEST MIRROR
ON THE IDENTITY.
ASSUME YOU ARE GOING TO
LIE TO YOUR SELF
AND YOU ARE GOING TO LIE
TO FUCKING EVERYONE.

Always Try to Remember that
First Clear Thought in the Morning.

If you are Getting High that Day
Remember
It's the only time before
You jump on the High Train that
You are likely to be Honest for a Flicker.

I believe that Pot does Not Control Us

It definitely is a flirtatious drug.

I LOVE POT.
IT SHOULD BE LEGAL ALL OVER THE WORLD.

I do believe it fucks up our memory.

I know kids get into it too young.

And I believe it's a Parent's obligation

And a Son and Daughter's Obligation

To be Honest.

Transparent!

Teach Control at the Earliest Age.

PILLS

PILLS

And More PILLS

The chances are, in the next 40 years there will be

A shit ton more drugs that will help everything from sleeping

to dreaming

Rebuilding Body Parts

Travel to

Other Universes yet to be Unlocked

New Highs

Along The Way

I think pills are like hot dogs or cured fast food meats.

They taste good going down but you have

No fucking idea what they are made of

Nor what they are really doing to your body.

They feel good in the first haze,

After there is an addiction to them because

They work and

We become dependent.

And they are coded to be addictive by their engineers.

We are all fucking lazy

Lazy with self-identity

Lazy with recognizing the signs our body sends us

Lazy with recognizing that we got

Too high

Too drunk

Too High to be High

Too Drunk to Drive

Too Fucked Up to Fuck

THE EASIER IT IS TO TAKE
THE MORE TO BE BEWARE.

TOBACCO

The most insidious of all the drugs

Like all our addictions, Tobacco is one that tastes great but really smells like shit.

It always amazes me how someone smells when they Jump into the elevator after just having had a Smoke.

Worse is when you stop smoking for a while and then just smell it and how bad it smells.

There is this bizarre consciousness that it is bad for us but

Our dumb fucking brain convinces us that

It is Desirable and

Delicious

How Easy

We Forget

Choking on the first cigarette

Riding in a car with a smoker

Throwing up on the first snort of Heroin

Burn of the straight Vodka shot

The Coke Bloody Nose

THE COMMON THREAD OF ALL HIGHS IS THEIR **SIDE AFFECTS SUCK.** AND WE LIE TO OURSELVES ABOUT ALL OF THEM.

Smoking smells great to the Smoker even though
It really Stinks.

ALCOHOL
Did you ever wonder if you really
Talked Too Much at that party
When you were Fucked Up?

That's another side of the
Party High.
Ever notice how
Fucking Dumb People Sound
When You are Straight and
They are all Drunk?

I am still trying to figure out alcohol.

I love Wine and
Love Good Wine More.
Love Vodka.
Love Great Beer.
Love Delirium.
I find the short high of
High Potency Beer to be
Unusually Delicious and Unique.

The trick with all drugs is to
Control our Conscious Reality
Who I really am and be Honest to Myself
about what I am really like
When I am Stoned or High.

It's one thing to get high
But to survive it is essential to
Strike Inner Personal Boundaries.

IT'S NOT JUST SAY NO!
IT'S ABOUT HOW TO USE **YES!**

One of the absolute boundaries is getting high to work.
Or worse, getting high on a break at work
and I'm talking mostly about grass.

If you are snorting coke at work,
You have a serious fucking problem and
Need Help from Yourself!

Chances are, if you are a pothead
You have blazed on your drive to work.
We've all done it.
Fuck—we are all still doing it.

The problem though is that even though pot illuminates
the creative juices,
It definitely fucks up your memory and concentration
and organization skills.

HEROIN-OPIATES

I am not going to talk about Heroin-Opiates.
It's a Killer and if you are reading this book and are taking H, or
Popping O's
Take a piece a paper Now and Write:
I am Fucked UP
I Hate Myself
It is Killing Me and
Everyone around Me knows I am Fucked Up
I need Help!

DRUG MANTRA:
► TIME AND PLACE RULES!
► FREQUENCY AND FORMAT
► INNER BOUNDARIES ALERTS
► WATCH WHAT I REALLY LOOK LIKE

Record myself talking stoned
Need to know what I really sound like when I am wasted
If I am doing it every day I am Addicted

STAY ORGANIC

I WANT TO SHARE THE NIGHT FLIGHT MISSION **I WROTE TO RELAUNCH THE BRAND IN 2016.**

I tempered the thoughts with a personal and humble touch, and one full of inspiration and hope. Missions are important to write down and memorialize, no matter what the project or relationship.

DEFINING OURSELVES
AND OUR PROJECTS IS CRUCIAL.

In June of 1981
When Night Flight first premiered
I held the strong vision that Night Flight would be
A Beacon of
Fresh, Cutting-Edge Entertainment.

When we first started, and for several years after,
I had the unique luxury to have
Total control of whatever we wanted to broadcast.
In fact, in the very beginning I can remember driving out to the
New Jersey uplink with the one-inch show masters myself.
In the early days of U.S. Cable there was
A Spirit that cable was going to bring something
Different and
Alternative.
In many ways this has proved to be true.
However, it was not very long until the execs at
USA Network became fearful of language
and other restrictive content.

That game changer happened one weekend when we aired the
classic music doc Rude Boy.
As I had previously distributed the film at midnight in movie
theaters,
I did not take the time to screen it and just put the uncut version
on the air...
Of course there is a good old
Rock and Roll blowjob scene in the bathroom!
I come into the office on Monday Morning and get all these
messages:
"Do you know what was on Night Flight this weekend?"
After that escapade, USA hired a Night Flight manager to
screen all our content before being shipped off.

The early years of Night Flight were the
Most fearlessly creatively free ones in my career.
There was a true sense of creative achievement and
I was very much aware that Night Flight was
providing a window to
A Greater Universe, to the Millions who had no idea that a
New Wave Punk scene was screaming from Los Angeles.
Or that Video was actually an Art Form.

CREATIVE FREEDOM IS NOT JUST THE ABILITY TO SAY **FUCK**

Creative freedom is not just the ability to say Fuck
whenever you want,
It is more a sense that programming choices are made
Not by commercial forces,
Not by analytics of taste,
Not by paranoia of getting kicked off the stage,
Not by fear of being taken to jail because of
acts of sexual innuendos and language.
The artist, whether
A painter
A musician
A comedian should
Start and End the
Creative Spirit with a pure sense that
He or she can allow their creativity to flow freely from the
creative heart
Without a personal or outside Censor.

I always felt the basic difference between the
Film and TV platforms, from
A creative point of view, was the
Degree and built-in state of
Creative Compromise along the process.

The beauty of Night Flight was that we were dedicated to
Exploring and
Discovering
New and Old
Eclectic Content
Without someone looking over our shoulders and telling us that
This was shit or
Not appropriate or
Too outrageous for broadcasting.
AND we had eight hours on Friday night and
Another eight hours on Saturday, so we could
Fill it with both long- and short-form delights.

We also felt that our programming mixes and
Contextual voiceovers were always from an
Educational and informative position.
To accomplish this huge amount of programming time,
we developed many sets of
Half-hour shows that were profiles on artists and
Thematic approaches to the music video medium and its artists.

Over the years, I personally became more aware of the
Night Flight influence on the '80s generation
Providing both inspiration and
The relief that the world was not flat.
That the Day the Music Died really never happened.

AN ANARCHIST SENSE
OF ENTERTAINMENT

I believe it comes down to

Discovery, and a sense of surprise

And an anarchistic sense of entertainment in a

Late Night Forum, immersed in a

Cultural Video Revolution.

A TV Journey to get high on.

The Wow Factor of

Artistic Discovery in

All its varied Glory is what

We aspire to and will get from Night Flight.

Night Flight will continue to embrace

The DNA of Nostalgic Content, both in a

Contextual format and in a Pure TV Streaming Format.

The good news for all of us Night Flighters is that we have

No Time Limit!

Fuck eight hours a night only on Friday and Saturday night.

The Internet has freed us!

No Censors.

And we are as Hungry Today

For something different yet familiar

As we were in '80s.

The Night Flight Library is a
Unique Cultural Time Capsule of
Artistic Youth and Expression
And for that we are so thankful!

IMPACT THROUGH CONTENT: ENOUGH CAT VIDEOS

There was another component to Night Flight, and that was
The DNA was Infused with
Progressive Social and Political Persuasion
We had fun with our political characters
Always in a good nature.

But today brings a higher meaning to our
Night Flight Nation.
And that is where
Impact comes in.
Impact is the heartbeat of Night Flight.
Great content always needs meaning that resonates.
That is why it becomes Great.

BUT NOW

We have to create a new video revolution!

For Today's Generation.

The Internet Generation.

The Global Hot Generation.

The Streaming Generation.

The You Want It

You Got It Generation.

The Global Citizen Generation.

The What the Fuck Are We Going to Do

If It's Already Too Late Generation.

My Dream is that the Impact Section

Will be a Beacon for Short Form Content for

Social Meaning and Progressive Grass Roots Stories.

Enough Fucking Cat Videos!

LET'S MAKE AN IMPACT THROUGH CONTENT

SMOKE NOSTALGIA

While we are on The Night Flight Journey

Enjoy the Nostalgic Flame from

The Hundreds of Artist Interviews

From the '80s.

They have a Rare Purity in Look and Quality.

The Heart Beat of Nostalgia is Precious

The Wonderful Emotions of
The Good Old Times.
It's Different for Every One Us
No Matter What Age
But the Feeling Is the Same,
Tied to
Music
Video
Concerts
Getting High with Your Older Brother
Knowing Your Mom or Dad
Were Getting Stoned and
Trying to Hide it.

Sneaking in the Basement
Stealing a Bud from Your Dad and
Hoping He Does Not Know.

NOSTALGIA IS THE BEST POT IN TOWN.

That's a Unique High on its Own.
That is what we want to
Embrace and Nourish.

SMOKE NOSTALGIA ON NIGHT FLIGHT!

SMOKE NOSTALGIA WITH NIGHT FLIGHT!

We promise to always
Endeavor to
Tie together the
Old and the New
And the Young and the Old

Soon, Surprise will be Embedded in the
Wall Mosaics in the TV Section.
And we are not going to tell you what's in them.

DISCOVERY IS OUR DNA.
HOPE YOU CAN
GET LOST IN THE DAZE.

DOPERS

ROPERS

HOPERS

SMOKERS

SCHEMERS

DREAMERS

From Dusk to Dust we try so hard
to achieve and be somebody.

TO PUBLISH AND BE PUBLISHED.
TO GET RICH.
MAKE HITS.
CLIMBING AND CLINGING CLOSE TO THOSE WHO HAVE HAD THE LIGHT AND TASTE OF THE TOP SEAT.

Smack, and all of a sudden over and over we are faced with the fragility and ridiculous of it all.

Where is the simple meaning of life without good health?

It's amazing how much discomfort is generated from the basic inability to take a good shit in the morning.

My father always snickered when he was older that having a good shit in the morning was one of the most important functions in life.

When we grow older, it's more common that we will touch the pain of loss through the death of our loved ones.

Strangely clear is that during those stressful life transitions, we have a heightened opportunity to really feel the power of the universe.

We go and work and
Try to Love,
Try to Succeed,
Try to Accomplish,
Try to Produce,
Try to Get Rich,
Try to Impress.

Even when we succeed by our own measurements, we usually
are not even satisfied by the standards of our measurement of
feelings and emotions.

And then the anvil of life slaps down the reality and quite easily
and with no reason whatsoever, the blacksmith of life simply
takes one fucking slap on the iron and its over.
Or worse we are fucked up and it's not over.

So, for a fleeting moment we feel the pain of loss for a loved one,
yet we return pretty quickly into the numbness of the urban
existence thereafter.
The moments of death are so precious for the living and the
DNA clock anesthetizes feelings of the death clock, so we can
return to our treadmill of the social success playground.

Remember the precious feelings and pain of loss.
Remember the few precious moments of death.
Therein lays the meaning of life.

IN THE REASON FOR DEATH LAYS THE RENEWED PASSION FOR LIFE.

GREAT GROWTH COMES FROM THE DEATH OF OUR BLOOD LOVES.

I SPENT MANY YEARS PROTESTING AND ORGANIZING CONCERTS AGAINST THE VIETNAM WAR.

My college graduation class almost cancelled our ceremonies because of the extreme social unrest in the spring of 1970. We all wore red armbands in protest with our graduation robes.

IT WAS A DISTURBING TIME IN OUR COUNTRY, BUT IT WAS ALSO A GREAT MOMENT IN HISTORY,

when we as youth and students were willing to go the extra mile, over the edge into harm's way for what we believed in.

To Protest

To Engage

To Activate our Will on the Nation

To Organize

To Unify as a National Identity

At my university, Union College, we were lucky to receive our hero, Mohamed Ali, on one of his speaking tours. He even visited our fraternity.

He was not just a boxing champion to us in the war movement.

He was a man of conviction willing to lose his most important treasure for his principle as a man.

His code of ethics was unconditional in the face of all forces beating at his virtue and talent.

WE ARE ALL TESTED IN MANY WAYS THROUGHOUT OUR LIVES. THE TESTS NEVER END

Sometimes small and petty

The More Successful and Prominent We Become,
The Bigger the Tests.

I have often used the words
PUPPETS OF POSITION
to exemplify the state of hypocrisy
that many politicians succumb to.
In many ways it is the brainwash we do onto ourselves that is
the root cause and effect of the political zombie inside us.

But it is really much more than just politics.
It's Friends
Family
Loved Ones
Wives
Husbands
Children
Parents

We Suck Ourselves into
Some Bullshit Rigidity of a Foundational Pattern of Belief

Unwilling to Challenge Ourselves

Afraid to Be Challenged
Ali is such a great guideline
Principles are Unconditional

But so is the willingness to accept that our principles may be torturously stuck in a Puppet Show that is NOT who we really are inside.

Not really honest

TO BE A PUPPET
OR
NOT TO BE A PUPPET

To be Willing to Self Challenge
Or to be caught in a
Web of a Frozen state of Old Fashion Ethics.

To be able to change and evolve as times open you up to new foundational ideas.

Ali was far from perfect as a role model.

We are All Hypocrites to some degree.

We are all subject to the imperfections of the nature
of man and woman.

We must be able to Stand Up to an Abusive Boss.

We must have the courage to lose our job
if it becomes unhealthy.

We must have the strength to believe we can succeed elsewhere
if we have to walk away.

We have to able to give up our title for no title at all,
if the company we are working for has transgressed

Our Ethics,
Our Principles or
Our Belief system.
Our Body
We are Judged by the Long Tail of our Personal Histories.

A SINGLE ACT CAN FORGE OUR HISTORY FOREVER WHETHER GOOD OR BAD.

The Wrong Impulsive Stupid Judgment and
Action Can Condemn us our Entire Life.

Discipline is Crucial.

Patience and Momentary Discretion are Foundational.

Train Our Instincts.

Trust our Intuition as a Natural State of Preservation.

WE ALL HAVE ALI IN US!
WE ARE ALL A CHAMPION!

We all have to Stand Strong and Face Off.

For What is Right

What is Honest

What is Transparent

What is Ethically Correct

What is Equal and Fair

WHAT IS COMPASSIONATE!

TO BE A CHAMPION HAPPENS

EVERY DAY
EVERY STEP
EVERY EMAIL
EVERY POST
EVERY THOUGHT
EVERY WORD
EVERY ACTION
EVERY BREATH

I SEE MY FATHER

PERCHED AT THE HEAD OF THE TABLE

PRINCE OF HIS FAMILY

POWERFUL IN HIS PRESENCE

LOVE OF FAMILY

LOVE OF THE TABLE

A LOVING WIFE AND MOTHER

AT SERVICE

TO OLD FASHION

WAYS AND CEREMONIES

THE SOUP IS NOT HOT ENOUGH BECOMES A YIDDISH JOKE REPEATED EVEN WHEN THE SOUP IS TOO HOT TO TASTE

How did the Soup

Become so Hot?

And Not Hot Enough?

Did we Learn

In a new

Generation

That words

And jokes

Caused pain

And loss of self

And diminished love

Did I learn Yet

Yes I learned

But still participate in
Unconscious actions
That repeat themselves
Without temper
Auto DNA
even though
I have Learned

The Soup is Always Hot Enough
Even when it is Cold.

How do those lingering
Loss imbeds of
Family
Father
Mother
Brother
Sister
Continue in the Clarity of Wisdom
Learned
Through Loss
And Lost Love

I was Beaten
Yet I Beat
I was Inflicted

Yet I Inflict
Beyond Myself

How do I Learn
When Not to Speak
Even though the
Soup May Be Cold
Or Too Hot
Or Too Salty
Or Too Sweet
Or Not Even There
Not on the Table
Not in the Fridge

Must Learn to Discipline
Myself from the Joke that Hurts
And Replace that Joke
with LOVE WORDS
That Heal and Sooth

So Easy to Hurt
So Easy to Stress
So Easy to Say
So Easy Not to Say

THE SOUP IS NOT HOT ENOUGH

Tell Me You Love Me
I Need to Know
Need to Hear Those Words
I LOVE YOU

So Hard to Repeat
So Easy to Say

NEVER HEARD THOSE PRECIOUS WORDS FROM MY FATHER YET I KNOW NOW HE LOVED ME

Why did they Have
Such Trouble
Just Saying
I Love You?

Did Their Parents
And Their Parents
Miss the Simple Impact
Or Realize
The Simple and Long Lasting
Absence of Impact

To Live a Life
In Pursuit of
Wanting to be Loved
By Words

When Actions may
Have told a Different Story
Not Understood

Tell Me You
Love Me

I NEED ACTIONS OF LOVE
I PURSUE HABITS OF LOVE

Words have
No meaning if
Actions and Habits
Sing a Different Song

Tell Me You Love Me
I need to Feel
Your Words Inside My Heart

Habits of Love
Sing their own Love Song
Flowers in Hand
Notes in the Bed
A Kiss
A Hug
First before
I am so tired

Words before Sleep
Words when Waking up
Words when Leaving
Words when Arriving

Smiling Faces
Even when Tired
Or Sore
Or Sleepy

Words of Love
Become Actions of Love
In Unison
Amplifying the
Sweet
Simple
Power of Love

Yes Please Tell Me
You Love Me

Tell me I Am
Number ONE

Tell me I Am
Your Soul Mate

Tell Me You Love Me
Forever
And Forever
After Forever

Love Me
But Don't Just Tell Me
You Love Me

Show Me You Love Me
With your Habits of Love

But Don't Forget
To Tell Me You Love Me
Every Time
All the Time
Forever and Forever

For I Love You
And I Love Me
And I Love Us
Forever and Forever

THINK OF YOURSELF AT YOUR AGE
NOW AND BELIEVE WITHOUT A DOUBT
THAT YOU ARE GOING TO LIVE IN GOOD
HEALTH UNTIL 120.

What preparedness should you make?
Think about living for another
90 to 100 years while you are
reading this book.
It is highly Possible.

MY FIRST THOUGHT IS LAND.

Second thought is Land that has Water, Sun, and good Earth

for growing

And won't be underwater in 50 years.

Or without Any water.

You don't want to just rent for the rest of your life?

Do you Really?

How many times will you fail?

How many breakups and

Divorces will you have?

How many Grand and Great-Grandchildren will

You be able to experience in Good Health?

Your children will most likely live even longer. (God Willing)

Chances are the Social Security blanket will not be the same and

And May not be reliable to sustain your financial baseline.

Energy will be Free and

Water expensive.

Society will produce more Free time and Less work.

Imagine now how would you live in a world where Energy is Free.
Travel is a fraction of time for long distances.

What is important?
Land
Earth
Water
Sunshine

Water will be complicated as it becomes increasingly harder to manage.
Dry rivers and Lakes
A national aquifer polluted for generations by mindless fracking.

Air most likely will become a controlled substance technology should solve.
Who knows, even water may have a technology savior before we all dry up from the lack of clean water.

Land that gives you an Organic Garden with Fruit Trees for Life.
Land with water that you have control over, from a healthy and protected aquifer.

But land that you Own,
Mortgage Free, will be the Most Precious Asset of All.

THINK HOW YOUR CREATIVE SPIRIT WILL BE FREE OF RESTRAINTS IF YOU DID NOT PAY FOR GAS OR ELECTRICITY OR A MORTGAGE.

So all I need are Food and Fun!

Love and Good Health.

It's a different dynamic.

I am afraid that land itself will become increasingly hard to purchase.

So you're 26, got a fair job, and $25,000 in the bank!

I say, figure out a safe spot in the country that has good soil and water and that you could see yourself living with your family if the urban scene gets weird.

Don't worry about it having a house. Prefabs are great now and very affordable.

New is better when it comes to the dwelling today.

Even though you may be an urban animal, you need some land to protect your longevity and your family.

THINK LONG!
CHANCES ARE
EVERYTHING
WILL HAPPEN.

EVEN THE
WALKING DEAD.

Where would you be?

Can you grow your food all year long?

Remember, travel will be quick and inexpensive because all energy will be renewable.

One acre of land can sustain a lot of food and shelter.

Make sure it's in a state that is against fracking cause that land and water will be polluted for your lifetime.

And be careful about the politics of the state you choose, as state and local politics will become increasingly more powerful and overriding.

RECENTLY I SPENT 3 WEEKS IN FLORENCE, ITALY, WRITING EVERY DAY SOME EXTRA CHAPTERS FOR THIS BOOK.

I wrote a chapter on David and Goliath sitting in front of the venerable masterpiece, pursuing the modern meaning of today's mythic struggle of the individual against the machine.

I WROTE AT THE TOP OF THE DUOMO BELL TOWER

about the Soup Never being Hot enough for my father.

I wrote on the top of the Leaning Tower of Pizza about trying to self identify each of us as our own Bell Tower in our community and our neighborhood.

I wrote in the Baptistery of the Duomo under Jesus how each and every one of us can make a difference and carry the message of Jesus in our habits.

I wrote every day mostly in poetic form and was hoping these final visions set in a land of renaissance would give a creative poetic ending to this book, using context as inspiration.

Luckily I typed and transcribed two chapters before I returned home, as I write in long hand.

The others are gone into the world of lost creativity.
Lost with those prints of films not preserved.
Lost with Digital Creativity that crashed without
backing up my computer.

I carried my precious manuscript on the plane returning from Paris to New York, planning on transcribing them while flying.

As life and the pursuit of perfection constantly delivers
its blows
I fucked up and left the manuscript on the plane.

The realization that they were left behind gave me a blow of pain and anger that shattered my heart
with a wrenching earthquake.

HARD WORK STUPIDLY FUCKED UP!

Creative Journeys rendered to another cosmos with only a glimmer of greatness…if only in my own mind's eye.

It's easy to rationalize that rewriting over again from scratch can always makes a work stronger and better…I wonder if true.

I tend to believe that great inspiration and spontaneity generated by special places and time lend to uniqueness that never are the same energy bond elsewhere.

Could the Beatles have produced Magical Mystery had they never lived in India?

When I produced Comedy's Dirtiest Dozen, a film that launched the careers of Tim Allen, Chris Rock and Bill Hicks, the magic of the performances were generated on a simple concept:

Prepare through extensive pre production an 8-minute set, but know that your filmed performance would be ONLY one take in front of a live audience with no retakes.

Each and every one of those 12 performances still possess a special edge and feel 30 years later...hopefully forever.

CREATIVITY HAS A DIRECT RELATIONSHIP TO THE MANIFESTATION OF CONTEXT AND IT'S IMPORTANT TO NOT ONLY RECOGNIZE THAT POTENTIAL BUT TO PRESERVE IT

Most of you reading this book will never write your messages in long hand and mail them in envelope with a postal stamp. All of us will have computers crash and lose documents and other precious files and photos.
Even in the New World Order of cloud back up how many times will you lose your phone and not have remembered to click auto back up?

Most likely in the near future everything will back up instantaneously
Including our conversations all day long.
Maybe even our thoughts that wiz by inside without being remembered will somehow get crystalized in some accessible cloud of spirit.

What I Do Know
What Will Never Change
What is Most Important
To Remember
Is That

WE ALL FUCK UP

We Fuck Up in Dumb Ways.
Sometimes We Fuck Up because we are Stoned
Sometimes from Arrogance and
Lack of Concentration.

Most of the time The Fuck Up is after
We have had the Awareness that is was in the
Process of Happening.

There is always the Speckle or Flash of Consciousness that
Appears Ahead of Time
Before Time has Elapsed the Vision.

The Vision
The Visualization
Is Always There
Before the Moment of
The Fuck Up.
Wisdom
Self Preservation
Awareness of Consciousness
Recording the Speckle of Unconsciousness
Are supposed to Kick In
To Prevent the Fuck Up.

But But But

The Little Shithead
Inside
Leads Us Astray

And it's always in a Split Second
That can Change your Life.

On the Road to Big Sur
Laurie left her scarf on the trail to the ocean from the highway.
Once we arrived in the motel many miles later,
she realized it was left behind.
Without hesitation I visualized that someone had found the scarf
and brought it up to the first stairs, and tied it to a post, so that
the owner would be able to come back and hopefully find it.

Maybe because it had already happened, I was able to receive the visualization and believe in the vision of success.

During my winding 30-minute drive to the location, I had numerous self doubts, and severe cruel self bitching moments, but I returned to the Self Visualization that
the scarf was tied and waiting for me.

HOW CAN WE POSSIBLY SUCCEED UNLESS WE BELIEVE

See

Visualize

Our Success

Whether a Moment away or Long range?

Yes!

The scarf was exactly where I had expected it to be.

But the scarf did not get there without a kind

Thoughtful

Caring

Responsible

Person.

That Act

That Person was the Basis of the Energy Trail

To Success.

That Person is Who We All Want To Be!
So that When We Fuck Up
Someone is There to Lighten the Blow
To Make a Happy Ending.

I Want To Be That Person
Who picks up the scarf and
Takes the Time
To Make A Difference!

I Want To Be That Person
Who Turns Around
After passing a needy homeless person and
Reaches into my wallet and gives a dollar.

I Want To Be That Person
Who after giving a dollar to that homeless person
Realizes that a $5 donation is
More Worthy at That Moment.

I Want To Be That Person
Who Apologizes to My Friend
Even though I truly believe it was
Not My Fault.

I Want To Be That Person
Who believes that Every Person
Deserves Proper Health Care.

I Want To Be That Person
Who stays Positive and
Hopeful
When technology is ruining my day.

I Want To Be That Person
Who has a fight with my wife over money
But
Works through
My Weaknesses and Insecurities
Overcoming Fears
To make Support
And Transparency
Triumph over Fear and Anger.

I Want to be That Person who has lived though
Arrorance and Negative Forces and
Grown Humble and Aware of My Weaknesses

I WANT TO BE THAT PERSON
WHO BELIEVES
SHE OR HE CAN MAKE A DIFFERENCE

MAKE A DIFFERENCE TO MYSELF
MAKE A DIFFERENCE TO FAMILY
MAKE A DIFFERENCE TO WORK
MAKE A DIFFERENCE TO COUNTRY
MAKE A DIFFERENCE TO THE WORLD

BELIEVE THAT ACTIVISM
IS SERVICE TO COMMUNITY
AND COUNTRY

WORK FOR A MORE COMPASSIONATE
SOCIETY UNTIL IT IS A FUNDAMENTAL
STATE OF AWARENESS

**I BELIEVE THAT I AM CONNECTED TO THE
UNIVERSE AND**

THAT ALL MY ACTIONS
ALL MY PURCHASES
ALL MY THOUGHTS
EVERY DOLLAR I SPEND
HOW I SPEND IT
IS MY VOTE
IS MY CONSCIOUS
IS WHO I AM
IS WHO I WANT TO BE
I AM WHAT I DO
I AM HOW I SPEND MY MONEY
I AM WHAT I EAT
I AM WHO I LOVE
I AM WHO I LIVE WITH
I AM WHERE I WORK
I AM WHAT I PRODUCE

I WANT TO BE A PERSON WHO. . .

► ANSWER THAT STATEMENT AND ASK THAT QUESTION

► WRITE DOWN WHAT YOU WANT TO BE

► WHAT KIND OF PERSON DO I THINK I AM?

► WHAT DO I DO THAT PRODUCES COMPASSION?

► WHAT DO I DO THAT PRODUCES ANXIETY?

► WHAT IMPACT DO I PRODUCE?

► CAN I FORGET AND FORGIVE WITHOUT HESITATION?

► HOW DO I FEEL WHEN I WAKE UP?

► HOW DO I REALLY FEEL WHEN I WAKE UP?

► DO I TELL MY LOVE ONES I LOVE YOU ENOUGH?

► MAKE YOUR OWN LISTS.

WE ARE THE SUM TOTAL OF OUR OWN ASSETS OF LIFE HABITS AND ETIQUETTE.

STAY HEALTHY
IN THE PURSUIT OF CREATIVE COURAGE
EVERY DAY

BELIEVE IN YOUR TRUE ESSENCE

LOVE THYSELF

TRUST YOUR IDENTITY

AND

LIFE WILL BE WHOLE
AND
SPIRITUALLY REWARDING

THE
GOOD GUYS
WIN
IN
THE END